Happy About® Working to Stay Young

Expanded Careers for Boomers and Seniors

By Jacky Hood

21265 Stevens Creek Blvd.
Suite 205
Cupertino, CA 95014

Happy About® Working to Stay Young: Expanded Careers for Boomers and Seniors

Copyright © 2007 by Happy About®

All rights reserved. No part of this book shall be reproduced, stored in a retrieval system, or transmitted by any means electronic, mechanical, photocopying, recording, or otherwise without written permission from the publisher. No patent liability is assumed with respect to the use of the information contained herein. Although every precaution has been taken in the preparation of this book, the publisher and author(s) assume no responsibility for errors or omissions. Neither is any liability assumed for damages resulting from the use of the information contained herein.

First Printing: August 1, 2007
Paperback ISBN 1-60005-035-2
Place of Publication: Silicon Valley, California, USA
Library of Congress Number: 2007929889

eBook ISBN: 1-60005-036-0

Trademarks

All terms mentioned in this book that are known to be trademarks or service marks have been appropriately capitalized. Happy About® cannot attest to the accuracy of this information. Use of a term in this book should not be regarded as affecting the validity of any trademark or service mark.

Warning and Disclaimer

Every effort has been taken to make this book as complete and as accurate as possible, but no warranty of fitness is implied. The information provided is on an "as is" basis. The authors and the publisher shall have neither liability nor responsibility to any person or entity with respect to any loss or damages arising from the information contained in this book.

Dedication

This book is dedicated to my mother Dorthey Pearl Templar Emmons.

Acknowledgment

My thanks go to many people. Mitchell Levy is a talented publisher, educator, business person, and human being. His decisiveness made this project a reality. Roger Smith, my long-time business partner, edited and encouraged throughout the project. Paul Highby joined Roger and me in finalizing the manuscript. More than 30 participants in several Third Stage of Your Career workshops inspired me to create this book. Frank Rosten and Pat Adrian sat through very long interviews and agreed to the short summaries. Al Wallace and Tom Jensen gave permission to use their stories. Daniel Dishno, Lisa Hendrickson and Jeff Rogers thoughtfully reviewed the book. Employment attorney Robin Bond discussed the book with me several times during its inception; she has added an excellent Foreword. Cate Carlson provided a meaningful cover design that emphasizes the variety of boomer/senior employment. My wonderful husband David Hood showed his usual amused patience when I added this book to my long list of other projects. To each of these people, I extend my deep appreciation.

A Message From Happy About®

Thank you for your purchase of this Happy About book. It is available online at http://happyabout.info/working-to-stay-young.php or at other online and physical bookstores.

- Please contact us for quantity discounts at sales@happyabout.info
- If you want to be informed by e-mail of upcoming Happy About® books, please e-mail bookupdate@happyabout.info

Happy About is interested in you if you are an author who would like to submit a non-fiction book proposal or a corporation that would like to have a book written for you. Please contact us by e-mail editorial@happyabout.info or phone (1-408-257-3000).

Other Happy About books available include:

- Tales from the Networking Community
  http://happyabout.info/networking-community.php
- Happy About Online Networking
  http://happyabout.info/onlinenetworking.php
- Happy About Tax Relief: The OIC Solution
  http://happyabout.info/oic.php
- Happy About People-to-People Lending With Prosper.com:
  http://happyabout.info/prosper/
- Overcoming Inventoritis:
  http://happyabout.info/overcoming-inventoritis.php
- Moving From Vision to Reality
  http://happyabout.info/myfaith/vision2reality.php
- 30-Day Bootcamp: Your Ultimate Life Makeover:
  http://www.happyabout.info/30daybootcamp/life-makeover.php
- Happy About Apartment Management:
  http://happyabout.info/apartment-management.php
- Confessions of a Resilient Entrepreneur:
  http://happyabout.info/confessions-entrepreneur.php
- Memoirs of the Money Lady:
  http://happyabout.info/memoirs-money-lady.php
- Happy About Joint Venturing:
  http://happyabout.info/jointventuring.php
- Happy About LinkedIn for Recruiting:
  http://happyabout.info/linkedin4recruiting.php

Contents

Foreword — Foreword by Robin Frye Bond, Esq. 1

Chapter 1 — **Work Longer, Live Longer** 5
- The Evidence Mounts: Working is Good for Your Health 5
- Sense of Purpose 6
- Self-Esteem 6
- Mental Focus 7
- Social Contacts and Social Presence 9
- Alternative Home 11
- Financial and Physical Ways in Which Paid Work Can Contribute to Your Health 12
- Work Longer, Live Longer 13

Chapter 2 — **Work and Grow Wealthy** 15
- The Beatles were Right, but Money still Matters . . . 15
- Salary vs. Retirement Income 16
- Too Busy to Spend 16
- Company Benefits that Save Money 17
- Get Paid to Meet and Interact with People 17
- The Money Value of Time 18
- How to Double Your Money 19
- How to Turn $1 into $75 in 5 Years 19
- Compound Interest Calculators and Other Useful Tools 19
- Building Your Pension 21
- Nice Work! 22

Chapter 3 — **You Are Needed** 23
- The Impending Shortage of Workers in North America 23
- Old West, Young East – For a While 25
- The World-Wide Labor Shortage 25
- Mature Workers Have More Education 25
- Why Does It Matter? 27
- What is Meaningful Work? 27
- Building Lasting Services 28

Options for Western Society in the Next
Few Decades ... 29
Importing Goods ... 29
Importing Labor ... 30
Offshoring Work ... 30
Improving Productivity ... 31
Increasing the Education and Skills of
Younger Workers ... 31
Employing Older Workers ... 31
Experience ... 32
Education ... 32
The Big Cost Question ... 33
Demonstrating this Reality to Employers ... 34
Passing Laws ... 34
Educating the Companies ... 34
Using Older Workers to Compete Successfully ... 35
You are Needed! ... 36

Chapter 4 Working for a Cause ... 37

Rationale for Retirement ... 37
Getting Paid to Further Your Cause ... 39
Working and Donating ... 40
Stay on the Job and Volunteer in Your
Spare Time ... 41
Marshalling Volunteers ... 41
Paid/Partially Paid Leaves of Absence
and Sabbaticals ... 42
Helping Your Company Help Your Cause ... 42
Company Foundations ... 43

Chapter 5 Staying with your Current Employer ... 45

Three Options for Postponing Retirement ... 46
Should You Stay With your Current Employer? ... 46
How to Stay with your Current Employer ... 47
Prepare in Advance ... 48
When Forced Retirement is Required by
Laws or Rules ... 50
Resist the Early Retirement Buyout ... 52
Your Job Has Been Eliminated ... 53
Grow the Job ... 54
Stay Put and Make Hay ... 55

Chapter 6	**Finding a New Employer** **57**
	Moving On 57
	Your New Job: Shopping for Your Next Position ...59
	Job Hunting Checklist......................60
	Interviewing 62
	Other Job-landing Approaches................64
	Big Problems 65
	You Can Do It.........................65

Chapter 7	**Creating a New Job** **67**
	The Typical Millionaire Owns a Construction Company...................68
	Free Lancer 69
	Almost a Free-Lancer...................69
	Small Business Owner 70
	Entrepreneur-ship.........................72
	Another Advantage of Going It Alone...........73
	Same Job, New Job or New Enterprise 74

Chapter 8	**Equal Time** **75**
	Doing It All 75
	One Hundred (Useful) Hours in Every Week 76
	Something Special Every Week...............77
	Something Special Nearly Every Day...........78
	Time Management 78
	Double Your Fun: Doing What You Want 100 Hours Per Week 80
	Final Message 80

Appendix A	**The Reality of Retirement** **81**
	Dream Retirements Down the Drain............81
	How do People Really Spend their Time in Retirement?.......................82
	Why so much Television Viewing?.............82
	Life-Threatening Addictions 83
	Will Volunteer Work Create A Successful Retirement? 84

Appendix B	**Overcoming Age Discrimination**	**87**
	Discrimination: Both Real and Imaginary	87
	Two Approaches	88
	Salary Discrimination vs. Age Discrimination	89
	Avoid the Kindergarten	92
	Fields that Love Gray Hair	92
	Homework is Critical to Success	92
	Take the Plunge	93
	Once You Are Hired	94
Appendix C	**Boomer/Senior Career Paths and Boosters**	**95**
	American Express Company	97
	CVS Pharmacy, Home Depot, Saks Inc., Toys "R" Us	97
	EDO Corporation	97
	Fujitsu Limited	98
Author	About the Author	99
	Success Stories	100

Foreword

Foreword by Robin Frye Bond, Esq.

Robin Frye Bond is the founder of the employment law firm Transition Strategies, LLC www.robinbond.com

Jacky Hood calls it as she sees it – and she sees a lot. Both as a college teacher and as a consultant to corporate America, Jacky has interacted with thousands of people from all walks of life grappling with the upheaval they experience in today's ever-changing world of work. She has helped people deal with downsizings, right-sizings, plant closings, relocations, new job offers that require taking a leap of faith, and often that biggest of all workplace decisions: is it time for me to retire? In this exciting new book, Jacky shares her wisdom in helping readers answer that last million-dollar question.

And million-dollar question it really is. As we Babyboomers live longer and longer, many of us are coming to grips with the financial reality that we need to defer retirement and work longer to maintain our standard of living. For a generation who embraced the ethic of overwork, another consideration about retirement occurs to us: are we really ready to throw in the towel, or do we have a lot of great working years, and ideas, still left to contribute?

Horace, the ancient Roman poet, said, "Adversity has the effect of eliciting talents which, in prosperous circumstances, would have lain dormant." Because my law practice is focused on helping clients deal with the changes – both positive and negative – that occur in employment situations, Jacky and I have had occasion to share ideas about how best to help individuals in times of job-related adversity. This can mean everything from helping someone effectively turn around a performance improvement plan with a boss that seems to be forcing them out, to navigating the stress of negotiations and successfully maximizing pay, perks and protections when clinching a new employment offer, or the ultimate challenge: what to do when a person's employment is terminated. In each of these times of change lies great opportunity. Depending on your perspective, you can see each of these life-changing event as the end of your world as you know it – or as merely the prerequisite closing of one chapter that is necessary before you can move on to the next exciting chapter of your life. What often makes the difference is the level of supportive resources the older worker feels he or she has in understanding what options are out there, and plotting a course through the choppy waters. Jacky's book is just the resource that is needed.

When an older worker comes to see me to review a severance package, it's often an incredibly stressful time, especially if he or she has had a long tenure with one employer and is unsure how to try to find the way in a new employment marketplace. The fear of competing with the young lions can often cause an older worker to think that opting for early retirement is the best bet. (At least it can initially seem like the most face-saving option, rather than trying to secure new employment, and facing the inevitable rejection that process always entails.) I am thrilled to see that a book like Jacky's is now available for these clients to provide both that positive inspiration, and critical guidance that encourages older workers to not give up, but rather to use their wit and wisdom to win in the world of work. Read this book before you decide on retirement, and learn how others have turned adversity into wildly creative and productive adventures in their later years of life. Jacky's stories echo what I see in my own practice about how Babyboomers are redefining the whole concept of "retirement" and keeping moving forward in novel and exciting ways that benefit not only themselves, but the rest of us as well.

There are tangible benefits to having a thriving senior population. Seniors create growth and wealth in the hospitality, travel, pharmaceutical, health, financial services, legal and housing sectors of the economy, to name but a few. Thriving senior markets not only create growth and economic vitality in corporate America, but seniors are increasingly becoming entrepreneurial, and bringing innovation and new growth in a variety of ways.

Whether teaching us how to stay with our current employers, find new ones, or pursue our passions through public service or entrepreneurship, Jacky's book is your guide to making the most of your talents, and finding that conviction and purpose for the exciting later years of your life. I encourage you to use this book to help those you love think through critical work junctures, and get a plan in place to recharge and retool before taking a position about retirement. Get ready, set goals, and achieve greatness!

Chapter 1
Work Longer, Live Longer

Emma Shulman has a problem that annoys her: excess energy. The 92-year-old social worker is employed by the New York University School of Medicine. She reports to Dr. Steven Ferris who says he would need to hire two or three people to replace her. Shulman says that for her, going to work is a vital part of staying healthy well past the standard retirement age. [1]

The Evidence Mounts: Working is Good for Your Health

Work seems to get in the way of your health: you feel you could exercise more, eat better, and escape stress if you could stop working. Surprise! People who continue to work for pay live longer, healthier lives than those who retire. How is this possible? The strongest reason may be that a sense of purpose promotes mental health. Mental health, in turn, promotes physical health.

---

1. Paraphrased from Peter Coy, "Old. Smart. Productive." *Business Week*, June 27, 2006, page 78

Sense of Purpose

All of us need to see our impact on the physical and social world. Younger workers are less able to choose work with meaning because they must focus on earning, learning, and building experience. Older workers can be selective in choosing work with a special sense of purpose.

Any job can have meaning if you think about what it produces and who benefits. Two people may appear to be doing the same task, but one is laying bricks and the other is building a cathedral. Constantly improving the products and services and making your work more efficient and effective reinforces your sense of purpose. Set yearly, monthly, weekly and daily goals that keep you looking forward. As boomers and seniors, we need to remind ourselves and those around us to look to the future.

Supposing you are waiting tables in a restaurant. Your goals might be:

- This year I will learn how to do the cashier's job so that I can fill in when needed or move into that position.

- This month I will make a well-thought-out suggestion to management to increase revenues or reduce costs.

- This week I will improve the layout of my locker.

- Today I'll thank a loyal customer.

Self-Esteem

Contributing strongly in a job or career strengthens your self-esteem. It reinforces your self-assessment as a competent person valuable to society and worthy of respect and financial compensation. On a daily basis, you find yourself planning, managing, creating, deciding, and influencing. You are surrounded by others who are also creating goods or services. You can be a role model for these people and you'll find role models among them. Others depend on your energy, effort, skill and wisdom. All of this raises your sense of self-worth.

Mental Focus

Like our bodies, our brains age. Not all the news is bad; prevailing wisdom was that the number of neurons was fixed early in life but recent research with stroke patients shows that new neurons can form late in life.

As the brain grows older, it undergoes complex and poorly understood changes — from the biochemical, to the molecular, structural and functional — that lead it to shrink. The brains of those aged 40 and older decrease in volume and weight by 5% every ten years. Much wisdom about the ageing brain has recently been overturned. It was thought, for example, that the loss of neurons led to forgetfulness, culminating in Alzheimer's disease. Researchers now blame the loss of synapses — connections between neurons. It had been thought that new brain cells grew only in young children, and that thereafter every bump on the head or glass of wine led to a loss of intelligence. Recent work has shown that, given intellectual stimulation, new neurons will grow in adults' brains. [2]

---

2. "Wisdom or senility," *The Economist*, February 16, 2006

To some extent, brain function is a matter of "use it or lose it." Reading, solving crossword puzzles, and other intellectual activities will stave off memory loss and other intellectual degradation.

Elderly adults who perform as well as younger adults on certain cognitive tests appear to enlist the otherwise underused left half of the prefrontal cortex of their brain in order to maintain performance, Duke University neuroscientists have found. In contrast, elderly people who are not high performers on the tests resemble younger adults in showing a preferred usage of the right side of the prefrontal cortex. The researchers said that, although their finding is basic, it raises the potential of using either training or drugs to enhance cognitive function in the elderly by increasing "recruitment" of the left prefrontal cortex.[3]

A Japanese entrepreneur introduced a game designed to increase the player's mental age: *Dr. Kawashima's Brain Training: How Old Is Your Brain?* Ironically, this game assumes that a higher age is better. Several million people have purchased the game and are delighted that the Brain Age rises with repetitive use. Several similar products have been introduced.

Though it may not hurt sales of these games nor diminish the 20 hours my husband spends each week on Sudoku, recent research says they may only improve one's ability to play the game.

---

3. Dennis Meredith, "Brains of Elderly Can Compensate to Remain Sharp," *Duke University News and Communication*, November 7, 2002

Learning how to play a new game or learning a foreign language do help, but repetitively playing the same games does not aid mental function in other areas. A great advantage of obtaining mental stimulus from work is that it constantly changes, especially if we set and achieve goals.

Of the nine easy steps to prevent mental loss cited by Tucker Sutherland in the April 27, 2006 issue of *Senior Journal*, several are even easier if we are working: mental stimulation, social network, physical activity, and avoiding alcohol and tobacco.

The trouble with retirement is there are not a lot of social or intellectual demands," says research psychologies Denise Park of the University of Illinois. Life becomes routinized," a recipe for cognitive decline. Some of the decline attributed to aging may therefore reflect not aging per se but factors much more within people's control.[4]

Social Contacts and Social Presence

Work provides a way for boomers and seniors to maintain social contacts on a daily basis, a very strong contributor to mental health.

It has been said that middle-aged people are invisible. It's easy to feel that way in a shop as the clerks talk with each other while going through the motions of serving customers. Many times, it seems highly unlikely that the person serving us will be able to identify us in any meaningful way after we leave the store.

---

4. Sharon Begley, "Old Brains Don't Work That Badly After All, Especially Trained Ones" *Wall Street Journal*, March 3, 2006 page B1, column 1.

This type of invisibility does not occur on the job. We are noticed by customers, suppliers, subordinates, and our bosses. In simple terms, psychological visibility is the principle that other people allow us to experience ourselves in a perceptual way. As psychologist Nathaniel Branden puts it:

> When others react to a man, to their view of him and of his behavior, their reaction (which begins in their consciousness) is expressed through their behavior, through the things they say and do relative to him, and through the way they say and do them. If their view of him is consonant with his own and is, accordingly, transmitted by their behavior, he feels perceived, he feels psychologically visible.[5]

While self-assessment of your own abilities, worth, and contribution should be the main factor in self-esteem, recognition by others whom you respect and admire contributes to mental health.

Structured Time

Day of the week, dates and even the time of day become blurred for those who do not work. Occasionally losing track of time can be refreshing and relieves stress. After a week or two however, unstructured days can lead to boredom, apathy and sleep problems.

---

5. Nathaniel Branden, *The Psychology of Self-Esteem*, page 201

Up to one half of elderly persons use some kind of sleeping medicine. The elderly are prone to develop sleep phase disorder and may sleep during the day and stay awake at night. It is unknown if such changes in the sleep patterns of older persons are due to alterations in circadian rhythm. More than likely the causes are multifactorial. Older persons may have unstructured days after they retire...[6]

Alternative Home

Home is a great place for sleeping, eating, and being with family. After about 80 hours per week, home is a dead-end. We get on our own nerves and those of our housemates. If we live alone, home can be a social place only if we entertain.

What's the alternative for the other 80 hours in the week? Clubs? Coffee shops? Libraries? Museums? Movie theaters? Athletic facilities? All of these are reasonable and all of these have limitations including cost and limited hours.

The workplace provides a great place to spend 20 to 60 hours each week. Not only are you welcome at work, you are paid to be there! The environment is as familiar as your own home. You can personalize part of the work place: your locker, your desk, perhaps an office. In many cases you can go to your workplace any time of the day or night.

Starbucks Corporation coffee shops have been one of the great business success stories of the past two decades. Dozens of copycat businesses are also doing well. The rationale behind the success of these shops is that they

---

6. Joseph A. Kwentus, M.D., "Sleep Problems," *Clinical Geriatrics*, August 2000

serve as a Third Place that is neither home nor office/school. If you retire, you'll have one less place where you feel at ease and welcome.

Financial and Physical Ways in Which Paid Work Can Contribute to Your Health

Drawing a paycheck rather than relying on pensions or savings gives you greater ability to pay for medical care, pharmaceuticals, sports, fitness, healthy food, and supplements.

In addition to wages, many employers provide complete or partial health insurance. A March 2005 AARP study found that 52% of people 50 and older who are working cited "need the health benefits" as one of the reasons. Though people without health insurance are not without medical care, those with insurance are more likely to seek and receive preventive care.

In addition, your employer may provide health sports/fitness facilities, lockers and shower rooms for riding/walking/running to work, health classes and counseling. Those employers who do not have facilities or classes onsite may subsidize outside sources. Choosing to walk, run, or cycle all or part of your commute is a very convenient way to obtain regular aerobic exercise.

Your work may also be physically demanding. Middle-aged and older people should consider physically demanding work in any career or job change. It's a great way to get and stay fit while making an economic contribution and earning money.

Company cafeterias often have nutritious meals at low prices. Carrying lunch to work is another way to eat healthy foods and save money. If your company does not have a refrigerator, point out to your employer how much time is wasted when people have to go to restaurants at lunchtime. Also, they come back sleepy and possibly slightly tipsy!

Perhaps most important, the work environment provides role models of people who are physically active and interested in nutrition and mental/emotional health. While there may be numerous conversations about illness at the local senior center, that's not the way to receive motivation!

Work Longer, Live Longer

Postponing retirement can mean a longer working life and a longer retirement.

For most workers, there is a widely held perception that spending more time on the golf course and less time at the desk will help you to reach old age. But research... has now suggested that early retirement at 55 may actually make you more likely to die earlier than if you had carried on working. The study, published in the British Medical Journal... found that workers who retired at the age of 55 had a significantly higher mortality compared with those who worked until 65. In fact, the death rate was almost twice as high in the first ten years. Factors such as gender and socioeconomic status were taken into account.[7]

---

7. Louise Gray, *The Scotsman*, October 21, 2005

Chapter 2: Work and Grow Wealthy

It's never too late (or early!) to begin investing. For a little inspiration, look to the amazing story of Anne Scheiber. Most people haven't heard of her, but she's one of the world's greatest investors. In 1932, Ms. Scheiber was a 38-year-old IRS auditor. Intrigued by the stock market, she forked over most of her life savings to her brother, a young stockbroker on Wall Street, who lost it.

Determined to try again, but this time relying on herself, she saved $5,000 and plunked it back into stocks in 1944 (at the age of 50). By the time she died in 1995 (at the age of 101), her money had grown to $20 million.[8]

The Beatles were Right, but Money still Matters

While "money can't buy you love," it certainly makes retirement more comfortable and fun. When you do retire, bring plenty of money. Delaying retirement allows you to live well now and save for the future.

---

8. Selena Maranjian, It's Not Too Late to Invest http://www.fool.com/investing/value/2007/04/24/its-not-too-late-to-invest.aspx April 24, 2007 (click on http://tinyurl.com/2okpbw)

Salary vs. Retirement Income

Few pensions provide the same income as working. Even more important, pensions seldom increase. That's where the term "fixed income" arises. Most salaries grow with inflation and growing in your job can increase your salary above inflation.

A person who retires at 60 expecting to live for 25 years on $30,000 a year -- in today's dollars -- of retirement savings will come up $358,000 short if he or she lives five years longer than anticipated, says Mike McCarthy, a financial planner with Hewitt Associates, Inc., a consulting firm in Lincolnshire, Ill. The projections assume an annual inflation rate of 4% and an annual return on investments of 8%.[9]

Too Busy to Spend

Think about how much more you spend on vacation than while working. Transportation, lodging, restaurant meals, and entertainment are expensive. The irony is these are much more attractive when they are rare. How quickly we miss our own homes and cooking! Better to have a few weeks of luxurious vacationing each year then 52 weeks of so-so travel and accommodations.

Even when not traveling, non-working adults fall into expensive habits: home remodeling, club memberships, hobbies, sports, and shopping for themselves and their children and grandchildren. Working people shop with a purpose and are less likely to come home with unnecessary purchases.

---

9. Melanie Trottman, *Does Living Longer Delay Retirement?*

Company Benefits that Save Money

Working adults receive many benefits that non-workers must buy. Your company probably provides free beverages. People who work in retail stores often get substantial merchandise discounts. Restaurant workers enjoy free meals. Some companies and institutions pay for uniforms. Office workers eat in subsidized cafeterias. Some companies pay for club memberships (business, airline, social, fitness) or provide fitness and sports facilities and social clubs. Many companies pay your normal salary when you are on vacation or sick; this benefit is worth 5% or more of your salary. Companies pay for required travel. If your business requires constant travel or overseas living, you may have no housing expenses.

Insurance of various types is probably the most valuable benefit many workers receive. Health insurance for doctors, hospitals, prescriptions, dental work, and vision care may be free or subsidized for the worker and even some dependents. Another popular benefit is a flexible spending account: pre-tax dollars for co-payments, eyeglasses, contact lenses, and over-the-counter medications. While you must pay for these items, you save 30-50%, depending on your state and income level, because no taxes are subtracted.

Get Paid to Meet and Interact with People

Most jobs provide an opportunity to meet and interact with customers, vendors, and other employees. A retired person must find these daily human interactions with friends, relatives, neighbors, or in clubs, religious organizations, political parties, or as a consumer.

Unfortunately many of these methods of human interaction are costly. Shopping tops the list both in stores and in hiring services such as housekeeping, gardening, home repair, fitness training, massage, hair styling, manicuring, learning music, and so forth. Joining clubs can also be expensive. Even volunteering for a political, social or religious cause can put you in the position of also contributing money to these groups.

Entertaining friends and relatives is also costly. Visiting them can entail expensive travel and the social obligation to reciprocate. Outings to sporting events, theaters, concerts, restaurants, casinos, and nightclubs deplete savings at a rapid pace.

Working people do all of these things but days or weeks go by in between. A non-working adult can spend as much on social interaction in a week as a working person does in two or three months. The working person obtains the psychological benefits of human contact on a daily basis. Interacting with family and friends and in outside organizations is a special treat.

The Money Value of Time

As you become older, you may feel like kicking yourself for not saving and investing at a younger age. It's never too late! The money value of time applies at 60, 70, or 80 just as it did at 30, 40, or 50.

The money value of time springs from the magic of compound interest. Money saved earns interest, dividends, or capital appreciation. The form of earnings is not important. The magic comes from saving the earnings and earning money in these ways.

How to Double Your Money

Open your purse or billfold and take out a $1 bill. Will you miss it today? Will you be glad to have twice as much in eight years from now? At just 8.5 % compounded monthly, a dollar saved today will be worth $2 in eight years.

How to Turn $1 into $75 in 5 Years

OK, you can't really do this in a risk-free way. What you can do with low risk is save an additional $1 each month and at the same 8.5 % have it turn into $75 in just 5 years. Think how easy it is to divert $1 each month from spending to investment: one fewer newspapers or cups of coffee. You can probably divert $1 each day. If you did that, you would have $2,258 in 5 years with such compound growth. Not bad, considering the very low impact on spending.

Compound Interest Calculators and Other Useful Tools

Handheld calculators that can compute compound interest are available from Casio, Inc., Hewlett-Packard Company, Texas Instruments Incorporated, and other companies. These devices cost $30 or more. If you would like to save that $30 (good idea!) use this table to estimate the growth in your savings. You will be able to save more than $1/month so multiply the numbers in the boxes by your monthly savings amount.

Table 2-1:

$1 saved monthly	5 years	10 years	15 years	20 years
At 5% interest or growth	$68	$155	$266	$407
At 10% interest or growth	$77	$201	$402	$724
At 15% interest or growth	$87	$263	$616	$1,327

If you use the Internet, there are many free sites available to help you save, invest and assess your wealth.

- Compound interest calculators are available at http://math.about.com/library/blcompoundinterest.htm and http://www.smartmoney.com/compoundcalc/

- This site constantly monitors the interest rates from banks and provides advice on where and how to stash your savings: http://www.mymoneyblog.com/

- Objective investment advice is available at http://www.fool.com/, http://www.morningstar.com/, http://www.smartmoney.com and http://www.kiplinger.com/

Choosing Investments for Safety and Growth

It's important to obtain the best rate you can. Bonds pay better than savings accounts or certificates of deposit. Stocks pay better than bonds. Risk goes up with better payout so be sure to diversify your holdings. Avoiding transaction fees and taxes also keeps the sum growing. Use discount brokers and keep your money in tax-free accounts like IRAs and 401Ks. Buy tax-free bonds when the rate is not less than 50% of the rate of taxable bonds. Another factor is holding the money in a currency that has a low inflation rate. There is no point in saving money if prices are skyrocketing in a particular currency; it makes more sense to buy goods or commodity investments.

Working people often receive several bonuses that help build their wealth. They may be in a pension plan that increases in value the longer they work. The employer may make saving easy and even match contributions.

Once you start watching your savings grow, you will start thinking of ways to increase the amount you save and invest. What better hobby than collecting money rather than buttons or stamps. You'll find yourself skipping restaurant beverages, reading rather than attending a movie, going for a walk instead of bowling.

Building Your Pension

In addition to building your retirement savings, continuing on the job can increase your pension and/or Social Security. Defined-benefit pensions pay a fixed amount that often increases with age or years of service. Defined-contribution plans grow just as savings do.

For U.S. workers, the age at which you can start collecting Social Security depends on your birth-year. As a first approximation, your Full Retirement Age (FRA) is 65 if you were born before 1937, 66 if your birth-year is before 1960, and 67 if you were born after 1960. The actual date to the exact month can be obtained from the Social Security Administration.

US Social Security pays more at FRA than if you retire in the three years leading up to FRA. The early retirement reduction in your payments is permanent. The penalty is 30% for retiring 3 years before FRA and it decreases the closer you get to FRA. If you retire early you may have to draw on your Social Security to meet living expenses. Keep on working and you can afford to wait for the higher payments.

Canadian Pension Plan (CPP) payments can start between the ages of 60 and 64. You qualify if you stop working or earn less than about $900/month for 2 months. Payments are permanently reduced if you choose to take this early retirement. After age 65, Canadians receive their full pensions with no penalty for working, although future earnings do not impact the pension amount. A big bonus for working seniors: Canadian Pension Plan payments increase by 30% if you delay your retirement until age 70.

Many private pensions operate in the same way: the longer you work, the higher your payments.

Nice Work! Build wealth while contributing, learning, and having fun. Take advantage of the perks that allow you to save and invest more. Nice work if you can get it! In the following chapters of this book, you'll learn how to keep your current job, find a new job, or create a job.

Chapter 3

You Are Needed

Having just passed through a recession and then a 'jobless' recovery, it is difficult to believe that the Western world faces a severe labor shortage in the coming years. This shortage means that middle-aged workers have the opportunity, perhaps even the obligation, to continue their careers far beyond established retirement age. This demographic trend can mean millions get a second or third chance to realize their career dreams. These dreams may have been pushed aside by the demands of supporting a family or pleasing an employer.[10]

The Impending Shortage of Workers in North America

Here are the non-intuitive facts for the United States:

---

10. Jacky Hood, Third Stage of Your Career, Training Class, January 2006

Within the next two years in the United States, there will be 151 million jobs but only 141 million people to fill them, according to the General Accounting Office. That shortfall is expected to grow as millions of workers begin to retire. Over a 22-year period starting in 2008, an estimated 76 million baby boomers born between 1946 and 1964 will leave the nation's labor force. But only 48 million workers under 40 will be available to replace them. Additionally, the number of workers over 55 rises to 31.9 million by 2015, up from 18.4 million in 2000, says the GAO.[11]

Anthony Carnevale, CEO of Educational Testing Service, says the US is facing a 14 million shortage of skilled workers by 2020. Job growth in the US is almost 2 million per year:

Between 1970 and 2003 the number of people employed in the United States rose by 58.9 million — a 75 percent increase.[12]

---

11. Diane E. Lewis, *Boston Globe*, 1/11/04
12. Olaf Gersemann, *Cowboy Capitalism*, 2004

Table 3-1:

Year	Needed Workers	Available Workers	Shortfall
2006	151 million	141 million	10 million
2020	179 million	165 million	14 million
2030	199 million	159 million	40 million

Similar situations exist in Canada, Mexico, and Western Europe. Japan is an exception.

Old West, Young East – For a While

Improvements in longevity combined with low birth rates have created the imbalance between young and old in the West. These factors are rapidly spreading to the entire globe.

The World-Wide Labor Shortage

The imbalance between East and West will be short-lived. The West should develop sustainable methods to provide goods and services and serve as role models to the developing world. These sustainable methods include increasing productivity, raising the skills of younger workers, and harvesting the education and experience of older workers.

Mature Workers Have More Education

In a reversal of the past, younger workers are less educated than the baby boomer generation. In a 2005 Congressional Hearing on workforce development, Steve Gunderson, Managing Director, The Greystone Group, Inc., provided these details:

- Of the 30 industrialized nations, the US ranks first on the percentage of 45-64 year olds with high school diplomas. But we fell to 5th place for those in the 35-44 age group with high school diplomas, and are down to 10th place for those between 25 to 34 age bracket with high school diplomas. We could wish the opposite were true.

- Seventy-five percent of all "new jobs" will require some level of post-secondary education. The trend is against us.

- The average job will last 3 to 5 years. After that, workers are dependent on flexibility and skills to find their next new job.

- The Urban Institute reported that only 68% of those entering high school four years ago have graduated; for communities of color the graduation rate is 50%.

- Data was released showing that of those graduating from high school and planning for Technical College studies,
  - only 10.8% have achieved Science Readiness
  - only 10.8% have achieved Math Readiness, and
  - only 36.4% have achieved English Readiness.[13]

The baby boomer generation has everything needed to step into the labor shortage: numbers, experience, skills, and education.

---

13. Steve Gunderson, Congressional Hearing, April 14, 2005

Why Does It Matter?

If a society has enough wealth to satisfy its needs, is it really necessary for everyone to work? Clearly it is impossible for most children and some adults not to produce. However, problems arise if a large percentage of society does not work.

Services generally cannot be stored and the US has a services economy. The dollar value of services has exceeded that of products. Worldwide, the production of services totals $21 trillion dollars.

Equally important is the psychological impact of lack of production. In Man's Search for Meaning, concentration camp survivor Viktor Frankl identified two primary sources of meaning: loved ones and significant work.

What is Meaningful Work?

For work to have meaning, it must produce lasting benefit. Any work that must be constantly repeated (building cars, mowing lawns, washing dishes, digging coal) is a prime candidate for automation. This frees humans to focus on work with lasting results.

How long? Work that last a few weeks, months, or years is better than work that disappears in a few hours or days. Even better is work that lasts for decades or centuries. I call this the Johnny Appleseed model of employment because some of the apple trees planted by John Chapman are still thriving after more than 200 years.

Building Lasting Services

How can a service become a lasting contribution? Creating lasting services will be the key to productivity in the future. New technologies assist the challenge. The ways to capture services include:

- Creating a digital copy of the service

- Developing and documenting the process of performing the service.

- Creating a tool that allows the service consumer to obtain the service without the human service provider

- Turning the service into a product.

Creating a digital copy of the service is the most interesting of these techniques because it applies to the performing arts. Story-telling, theatrical plays, dances, and musical performances of all types can be captured in video and audio format and preserved for decades, even centuries.

In more mundane services, developing and defining the process allows the transfer of the knowledge and provides a convenient mechanism for improving the service. Much of the current quality movement centers on defining processes.

The third method for capturing services is to create a tool that allows the service consumer to obtain the service without the human provider. Self-service gas pumps, automatic teller machines, and Web-based support are examples.

Turning a service into a product is a variation on the other three methods. The example that will have the greatest impact is turning live education into a stored product. While books have existed for centuries and self-study guides for decades, the confluence of computers and telecommunications will soon revolutionize education.

Options for Western Society in the Next Few Decades

For the next two or three decades, Western nations can meet the worker shortage by importing goods, importing workers, or offshoring work. After that time period, the only global choices will be to improve worker productivity, upgrade underskilled workers, and convince older workers to stay productive. A major purpose of this book is to illustrate the relative benefit of older workers vs. the other options.

Importing Goods

Trade is good. Generally it benefits both parties and increases total wealth. This is because we all need a variety of goods and services. We would rather have a pair of shoes and a pair of socks rather then two pairs of either. So swapping shoes for socks increases the standard of living of both traders. The same is true for nations.

To smooth trade, money is used as a means of exchange. Generally, money has no inherent value. It can't be worn, eaten, or used for entertainment. Problems arise when trading stops after the first exchange. If Asia has goods or services and the Western World has money, a sale can take place. Now, Asia wants to buy goods or services with its new money but it cannot. Similarly, the Western world wants to buy more goods and services from Asia but it has run out of money.

The Western world buys far more goods from Asia than it sells. This leaves Asia with Western currencies and the Western world broke but wanting more goods. Often this is characterized as a tragedy for the US. In fact, this problem is worse for Asia than for the US because we have acquired useful goods/services while those societies only acquire money.

Why the imbalance? It happens because Asia can produce higher quality goods and services at a lower price than can be done in the Western world.

Importing Labor

So why worry about a Western labor shortage? Why not simply fill it with immigration? This is a partial solution. However, today's immigrants to the US have different languages, values, cultures, politics, and religions than past immigrants did. Entire families want to immigrate, not just young adult workers. Older immigrants add to the welfare burden and their children require education.

Even more disturbing than these problems is the loss of the best and brightest from Asian, Latin American, and African nations. This loss exacerbates the young/old imbalance and the impending worker shortage in those countries. Some migration is very healthy; it promotes peace and understanding among the World's people.

Offshoring Work

Buying services in Asia and Africa is similar to importing goods. The Western world receives the benefits of the work and Asians end up with

Western money. The same business reasons compel offshoring and the same imbalances occur.

Offshoring is not the same as outsourcing. Outsourcing is simply the purchase of services by a company. All companies purchase a variety of services: legal, accounting, janitorial work, security, and so forth. The most successful companies focus on their core competencies and outsource everything else.

Most US outsourcing contracts go to US companies.

Improving Productivity	Technological and management advances have made possible a world that sustains six billion people. While those who oppose productivity improvements receive a lot of publicity, most humans embrace this form of progress. Improved productivity makes meaningful, long-lasting work possible.
Increasing the Education and Skills of Younger Workers	While we cannot increase the number of people between the ages of 10 and 50, we can increase their education and skills to produce lasting products and services. This is the recommendation of Anthony Carnivale, who does not see longer careers as a viable option.
Employing Older Workers	Compared to the other three options we've considered, keeping older workers on the job longer offers many advantages. Older workers provide knowledge, experience, loyalty, attendance, and wisdom. They know what needs to be done and they do it correctly. Inexperienced

workers may be quick and work long hours but they make many mistakes, are often absent and their turnover rate is high. Workers in mid-career have heavy outside responsibilities due to children. Older workers can focus on their jobs and careers.

Experience Older workers generally have a great many years of experience, much of which is relevant and up-to-date. Even those who left paid work to raise families, to travel, or to nurse elders, have 40 to 50 years of life experience.

Education Older workers did not split genes in high school nor did they study nanotechnology in college. However, more baby-boomers finished high school and more have undergraduate and graduate degrees than younger workers. Also, mature workers were educated when schools in the US had fewer problems with violence and overcrowding. Discipline was strong, social promotions rare, and grade inflation non-existent.

In Kramer vs. Kramer, the man contemplating loss of custody of his son listed all the advantages of losing custody but could only think of one disadvantage: his love of the boy. This outweighed a much longer list.

Here the weighty disadvantage to employing older workers is the huge cost savings of importing products, importing workers, or offshoring the work.

The Big Cost Question

All companies must constantly ensure that long-term revenues exceed long-term costs and that profits provide a market rate of return on invested capital. Generally, cost cutting is a poor investment.

The cost differences are substantial. Workers in India and the Philippines are paid less than US workers. Franklin Bank finds workers for $2,500 per year. Even though these workers are not doing a particularly great job, at that cost Franklin can afford to bring them to California for extensive training. California has a minimum wage; however, not many Californians can afford to work for minimum wage. Immigrants are among the few who are able to work for minimum wage.

So how viable is the use of older workers vs. offshoring? Or vs. immigration? Must older workers accept $2,500 per year in order to compete?

Here are the factors that make it possible for older workers to compete successfully with immigrants and offshore workers, even at substantially higher salaries:

- Offshore salaries are rising.

- Offshoring entails substantial non-salary costs including:
    - Establishing a subsidiary overseas or locating and contracting with an overseas company.
    - Acquiring and training offshore workers.

Demonstrating this Reality to Employers

There are three primary ways to demonstrate to companies that employing older workers is better for the bottom line than importing workers or offshoring:

- Pass laws
- Educate the companies
- Compete successfully against them

Passing Laws

Passing laws has many disadvantages. It violates property rights and ultimately it fails because companies choose their geographies and will move to those states, provinces, and countries that regulate and tax the least.

Educating the Companies

Company educators include:

- Business schools
- Non Governmental Organizations (NGOs) such as Civic Ventures
- The Press
- Books
- Shareholder pressure
- Customer input
- Unions
- Demonstrations; boycotts (activism)

Using Older Workers to Compete Successfully

Some companies have seen the light and realize they can tap into a loyal, experienced, well-educated workforce and beat the socks off the competition. A British organization surveyed the field:

> *FiftyOn recently conducted research through NOP which showed that employing the over-fifties can also enhance the reputation of the company doing so. Key findings of the research were:*
>
> - *83% think that employing older people is good for a company's image;*
> - *75% agree that older people tend to be more honest in the advice they give and aren't so interested in a quick sale;*
> - *89% agree that retraining is not a problem for older people and that they are able to take on new skills.*
>
> *This last point was supported by earlier research carried out for FiftyOn, which illustrated the growing propensity for older people to take on new IT skills. Over 4 million people over fifty own a computer and more than half of these regularly surf the Internet. Not only are these skills relevant to business, they scotch the myths that ageing leads to mental or creative decline. Diversity helps by creating a workforce that is representative of the wider community and one that increasingly mirrors the customer base of the business.*[14]

---

14. Recruit.net Newsletter, Issue 51, http://www.ukrecruiter.co.uk/recnet/rn51to60.htm

You are Needed! The western world faces a severe labor shortage in the coming decades. We can offshore more jobs, import more workers, or convince workers to retire later – including you! It's almost unfair to society for you to withdraw your talents in a time of need.

Chapter 4
Working for a Cause

Frank Rosten has had a fascinating career, or set of careers. He worked in quality control in the UK and then in Canada. Under a Canadian government contract with McMaster University, Rosten was sent to Latin America. When that project ended, Frank stayed on as a reporter for the Peruvian Times. He then immigrated to the USA and made strong contributions in aerospace and in technology transfer to the private sector including dental materials. Frank retired at 63 and volunteered for AARP and the Globe program. Now Frank is again being paid for his time selling nutritional supplements. He was recently elected to the California Senior Legislature as Senior Assemblyman for Santa Cruz/San Benito counties.[15]

Rationale for Retirement

Many baby-boomers and seniors are passionate about political, social, religious, or cultural causes. They long to divert the energy they pour into their careers to change the world. They may not realize that working for pay is a better way to accomplish this goal. Our society assumes that

---

15. Jacky Hood, Interview of Frank Rosten, March 21, 2006

people willing to work without pay are capable only of menial work and will be happy to perform low-level tasks.

Dorothea Glass retired as chair of a medical school department and moved to the ocean. She approached a local hospital with the offer to put her decades of experience as a physician and medical executive to work – for free. The hospital offered her a volunteer job filling water pitchers.[16]

So Dr. Glass went back to paid work at the Miami Veteran's Administration hospital, the American Congress of Rehabilitation Medicine, and at the University of Miami. Three organizations and countless patients, students, and physicians profited from her knowledge skill and experience.

Too many retirees, when donating their time and energies, are falling into dead-end jobs... Rita Vance retired three years ago. With 30 years experience in social work at non-profits and government agencies, she relished the idea of sidestepping the meetings involved in such settings and spending all her time with people in need. Instead, her first foray into volunteering found her sitting in meetings... and dishing up cafeteria-style meals at a senior center.[17]

---

16. Civic Centures Website: http://civicventures.org/publications/books/primetime_Dorothea-Glass.cfm (click on http://tinyurl.com/3x84e5)
17. Kelly Greene, Avoiding the Volunteer Trap, *Wall Street Journal*, April 24, 2006, Page B1

Ms. Vance had done far more for needy people in her paid work than as an unpaid volunteer.

Getting Paid to Further Your Cause

Most political, social, religious, and cultural organizations have paid positions. Managers, directors and other staff members set the direction for the organization. They supervise the volunteers and manage the budgets. You can have a far greater impact in a paid position than as a volunteer. In addition, you will maintain and improve your career skills and build your contacts.

Causes seldom pay private sector salaries, though some not-for-profit organizations have comparable compensation.

While a job in a cause may not offer the financial rewards of private-sector employment, the challenges are often greater. Imagine the difficulties in managing a children's sports organization. You must deal with several layers of government, public and private schools, parents, sports associations, equipment vendors, gymnasium/playing field/arena owners, fans, the press, numerous volunteer or paid time-keepers, judges, and coaches as well as the children who participate and those who are eliminated. This will make your previous industry job seem easy. Should you decide to return to the private sector at some point, you will have built a wealth of planning, negotiating, selling, coaching, and accounting skills.

Similarly, should you run for political office, you'll be working with a political party at national, state, regional and local levels, campaign staff and volunteers, and selling yourself to voters, endorsers (companies, unions, newspapers, blog writers), funders, and the press. If you are elected, for example, as mayor of your town, the challenges will grow.

Perhaps your cause does not yet have an organization and you choose to start one. From day one, plan to be paid as soon as possible. Volunteer your time but protect your savings. Causes can make money in many ways: fees for services; memberships; donations from individuals; and grants from corporations, unions, and governments. Forming a non-profit corporation takes effort and time but opens the door to many of these income sources. Non-profit corporations are allowed to pay market salaries. As founder and director, claim a reasonable salary. If you do not need the money, donate it back to the organization.

Working and Donating

Many factors can prevent you from working in a paid job for your cause:

- You live at a distance from the organization's paid positions.

- Your job skills differ from those needed. Perhaps you are a veterinarian and your favorite cause is a history museum. You could volunteer in a low-level position but do not have the qualifications for a decision-making role.

- You love your for-profit career.

In these situations, keep working and contribute money to the cause. If you need your income for living and saving, put the organization into your will.

Stay on the Job and Volunteer in Your Spare Time

"If you want something done, ask a busy person to do it." This cliché shows why a working person may contribute more to a cause than a retiree. If you care about a cause, you can volunteer 20 or more hours per week while holding a full-time job. This is true even if you are in a profession that demands 50 or more hours each week. You can do anything, but you can't do everything. To work full-time and volunteer half-time means that you need to spend less time watching TV, sitting in coffee shops, reading magazines, and taking naps. Is this a big sacrifice for your health, wealth, and changing the world?

If your income and savings are adequate and you care more about the cause than your paid job, change the ratio from 2:1 work-to-volunteer to 1:2. Remember that it's critical to continue doing paid work because it keeps your skills sharp and gives you respect among other volunteers as well as from the people the cause seeks to influence. When you hear a message from a working adult about a political stand or charity need, are you more inclined to listen than to a retired person? Other voters, donors, and the press feel the same.

Marshalling Volunteers

Many causes require a small army of people for a short time: cleaning beaches, building trails, and serving holiday meals. Employers are able to muster volunteers for efforts of this type. Boomers thinking about retiring to help a cause should consider staying with their employers and organizing volunteer events.

Paid/Partially Paid Leaves of Absence and Sabbaticals

In the 1980s, I was fortunate to work for ROLM Corporation. This company offered 12 weeks of paid sabbatical every 7 years of employment. Many employees used this time to help a cause. After IBM purchased ROLM, an IBM engineer joined my group. He had served in the Colorado legislature for seven years while on the IBM payroll.

Helping Your Company Help Your Cause

Louis Gerstner and Warren Buffet disagree. Mr. Buffet, Chairman of Berkshire-Hathaway, Inc. and one of the world's richest individuals, believes that corporations should stay away from causes. They should return maximum earnings to shareholders and pay employees fair wages. Then shareholders and employees can contribute to their own causes.

Mr. Gerstner, former IBM Corporation and American Express Company CEO, believes that there are ways that private industry can help a cause that charitable organizations cannot. While he was in Chairman of American Express, the company donated money from each local credit card transaction to local charities. Jerry Welsh who was Senior VP of the company said "We were giving money away, but were doing it in a way that builds (local) businesses and helps the cause." It also helped American Express. Gerstner said, "We now know we can do well by doing good." In addition to these quotes and information about several American Express charity efforts, Jocelyne Daw discusses similar programs by Lee Jeans, The Coca-Cola Company, Ford Motor Corporation and other companies in her book.[18]

---

18. Jocelyne Daw, Cause Marketing for Nonprofits, Wiley & Sons, 2006

Similarly, Deutsche Lufthansa AG's employees have formed a charity to help countries to which the airline flies. The employees perform volunteer work and they also collect the coins that travelers from country to country accumulate. These coins cannot be exchanged for the home currency so it is better to donate them rather than toss them into a drawer.

Two areas in which private industry should take a stand are free enterprise and free trade. The enemies of economic freedom make a very loud noise and have much of the press on their side. Recently I visited the United Nations complex in Geneva. There I was shocked to hear that non-government organizations (NGOs) such as charities and political causes can be official observers to commissions and participate in the discussions. Private companies cannot.

Company Foundations

The employees of the more than 2,500 corporate foundations are often on the same salary scales and receive the same benefits as employees in the for-profit part of the company. Corporate foundations are especially diligent in ensuring that their donations are well placed. Corporations support a variety of causes so you are likely to find one whose philosophy you support.[19]

---

19. http://foundationcenter.org/findfunders/statistics/pdf/02_found_growth/01_04.pdf (click on http://tinyurl.com/2ns3rf)

Chapter 5
Staying with your Current Employer

For Pat Adrian, Editor-in-Chief of Bookspan's The Good Cook book club, there is very little separation between work and life. She is always working on, thinking about, shopping for, or preparing food. Pat started her career as a copy editor for the Book-of-the-Month-Club catalog. A supervisor believed she had a talent for management. So, Pat read enough business books to be the equivalent of an MBA. She was given a choice of managing two new book clubs: one for cooking and one for business. She made the correct choice because the business book club folded. Business books become obsolete too quickly. Pat loves her work and thinks it's important to be earning. "I like that paycheck." The high point in her career was the Editor of the Year Award from the James Beard Foundation. When she finally leaves the book club, Pat plans to be a consultant on cookbooks including cover designs and recipes.[20]

---

20. Jacky Hood, Interview of Pat Adrian, January 27, 2006

Three Options for Postponing Retirement

Now you are sold on postponing your retirement for years or decades. The first step is deciding whether to stay with your current employer, move to a new employer, or go out on your own.

This chapter provides assistance in holding onto your current position and increasing its value. Chapter 6 outlines strategies for moving to a new employer and Chapter 7 helps you become an independent worker.

Should You Stay With your Current Employer?

Continuing in your current job is by far the best option if you can answer "yes" to five or more of the following questions:

- Do you love the job?

- Do you feel great loyalty to your current organization?

- Do your organization's products and services have a positive impact on the world?

- Do you have strong relationships among the employees, customers, and suppliers?

- Are you recognized for your contributions, knowledge, wisdom and skill?

- Have you worked to achieve a position that would be difficult to easily match in another organization?

- Would you be unable to match the salary you receive in another organization or on your own?

- Does your organization provide benefits that you need or want?

- Will your retirement benefits increase substantially if you stay?

- Would it be difficult to port your retirement benefits to another organization or self-employment?

- Are you working for the only suitable employer in your geographic area and are you unwilling to relocate?

Even if you have a large number of positive answers, you may want to consider the other options described in Chapters 6 and 7; you may decide that the grass really is greener.

How to Stay with your Current Employer

Even though your organization recognizes your value, that does not guarantee that it wants to continue to employ you. Unfortunately, your organization may encourage or force you to leave for any of the following reasons:

- Your profession has a legal mandatory retirement age (for example, if you are an airline pilot).

- Your organization is downsizing or reorganizing due to economic problems.

- Your organization has dropped the products or services with which you are associated.

- The industry has changed and now requires new or upgraded skills that you do not have.

- A new executive has come on board who wishes to surround himself with colleagues from a previous position.

- Your organization is moving to a new location (perhaps due to acquisition by another company) and paid relocations are not available. If the move is to another country, it may not be legally possible to transfer workers.

Unfortunately, older workers often seem to be singled out when a reduction in force is necessary. Employers often perceive that older workers:

- Are paid more (because of promotions or seniority)
- Drive up health insurance costs
- Have higher absenteeism
- Will not work overtime
- Have outdated skills
- Are unwilling or unable to learn new skills
- Are not worth training because they retire soon
- Will not be willing to relocate

While many of these perceptions are false, feelings are facts. When the decision makers hold these beliefs, it is necessary to change their minds or work around them. Appendix B outlines ways in which you can avoid age discrimination and avoid practicing it!

Prepare in Advance

The best time to defend against retirement or layoff is right now. The first step is to understand the relative importance of various aspects of your current job. Check one column for each row in this table; add other items of importance to you.

Table 5-1:

Current Job Aspect	Need	Want	Don't Care
Function			
Title			
Staff			
Salary			
Health Benefits			
Retirement Benefits			
Co-Workers			
Location			
Physical facilities			

Now consider whether your position is fairly bulletproof. If your organization suffers financial setbacks, what would be the order in which positions would be eliminated? What if your organization merged with another larger company?

There are no totally safe positions; however, Sales and Operations are safer than other areas. Companies must sell and produce products or services. In the short term, they can survive without marketing, product development, human resources, many administrative services, and training. These staff functions are the most likely to be considered redundant in a merger. Information Technology must continue during a downsizing but it may be scaled back or outsourced.

Within functions, the positions that survive downsizing are usually at the top and bottom; middle managers are pushed out. If you are a middle manager, make sure you keep up with the skills of the individual contributors. Even if you are never forced to be a front line producer again, you'll be a better manager.

In mergers, executives and top-level managers are the most vulnerable.

Can you move to a safer position in your organization without giving up your needs and most of your wants? How likely is a downsizing or merger? Prepare now to be able to move or make the move in advance.

When Forced Retirement is Required by Laws or Rules

Like many pilots, Captain Joe Spencer was forced by the Federal Aviation Administration (FAA) to retire from US Airways because he is turning 60. Captain Spencer is unhappy about the forced retirement partly because he will miss his colleagues.[21]

One way Captain Spencer could have stayed with his US Airways colleagues and continue to build his seniority would have been to learn to 'fly

---

21. Paraphrased from Jeffrey Laslow, "Final Flights: Retirement Rituals Soften the Bittersweet Side of Leaving a Career," *Wall Street Journal*, February 2, 2006, page B1

a desk'. He could have obtained an MBA. The FAA does not ground non-flying airline personnel.

Many pilots are protesting the age 60 rule.[22]

> Seventy-five years ago in a different era and a different country, Frederic Franklin began his dancing career - a career that continues today. Franklin, 92, who is a native of Liverpool, England, visited the University of Oklahoma School of Dance this week to observe classes and speak about how the dancing profession used to be. Will Franklin retire now that he is 92? Asked about closing the curtain, Franklin assured it wasn't going to happen. "Dancers don't really retire," Franklin said. "They come out and teach or produce, so they're always doing something. I just go out there and perform and I love it. I've had a long run and it's still going. While I still can, I will continue."[23]

If your job has a mandatory retirement age, you are probably well aware of it. Look around in your organization for opportunities in areas without forced retirement. If this is simply not an option, work with others in your profession to change the requirement. Find out when the rule was made and look up life expectancy at that time. Today a 65-year-old can expect to live until at least 80. In 1950, the expectancy was age 77.5. So, a mandatory retirement age set in 1950 should be increased by 2.5 years. When health or safety of

---

22. http://archives.californiaaviation.org/ pilot/msg00107.html (click on http://tinyurl.com/2orv2c)
23. Althea Peterson, 75 years later, he's still dancing, The Norman Transcript (Norman, OK) October 08, 2006, http://www.timeswv.com/seniors/cnhinsseniors_story_281214245.html (click on http://tinyurl.com/27xxva)

customers and others demands specific cognitive or physical abilities, these should be the determinants of forced retirement, not age.[24]

Resist the Early Retirement Buyout

Most companies don't want to force people into a layoff. The standard practice is to induce people to take a package of benefits and compensation. This is similar to airline ticket agents offering incentives for people to skip an overbooked flight. The longer you wait, the sweeter the offering will be. In some companies, the offers are usually backed by a threat that such packages will shrink in the future. It's a game of liar's poker and you'll need plenty of savvy to know when to stay and when to run!

If the early retirement offers succeed, there may never be forced layoffs. Because you have decided that staying with your current organization is the best or only working option for you, be prepared to resist the offers. Be very aware of your personal financial situation by answering these questions:

- What assets do you own?

- Which of these assets generate income (rents, interest, dividends)?

- What other sources of income do you have (family members with jobs, alimony, insurance settlements, lottery winnings, retirement benefits from previous jobs or the government)?

- What benefits will you receive if you are laid off in the future?

---

24. http://fathersforlife.org/population_politics/US_population_figures_80-96.htm (click on http://tinyurl.com/36mxjg),
http://www.efmoody.com/estate/lifeexpectancy.html

- How much income could you acquire from new employment?
- What are your current expenses?
- How much could you reduce your expenses with little change in life style?
- How much could you reduce your expenses in a real emergency?

Now you'll be much better able to assess the value of a retirement package. At first glance, the prospect of receiving a lump sum of a few months' salary plus outplacement services may seem extremely attractive. On further examination, you discover that your job search and possible relocation will take longer and cost more than the package. Similar outplacement services are available from federal, provincial and state agencies; you've already paid for these with your taxes.

Say "no" to the package, start saving, and become the most valuable employee in the company. During downsizing and mergers, many employees are distracted by the confusion. It's a great time to shine as one of the few employees focused on customers and the future.

Your Job Has Been Eliminated

Before this happens, have in mind several other places in the organization where you can make a strong contribution. One middle manager whose job disappeared pointed out to his organization that he is fluent in Mandarin and could help the company expand into China. His company not only kept him on, but also gave him a promotion. Don't assume that your managers know all your strengths and skills.

Grow the Job

It's not enough to just stay with your employer; you need to seek advancement and growth. Stagnation leads to layoff and defeats the purpose of working to stay young. The health and wealth benefits accrue only if you are stimulated and constantly learning.

Working for promotion is one way to grow. If you already know every aspect of your own job, learn as much as you can about the jobs of your co-workers and your manager. Active listening and observation are the best way to do this without being a nuisance. Generally, others will be flattered by your interest. Take training classes or read about the skills you need to do your manager's job.

Moving into your manager's position is not the only way to advance. Check the positions that are peers to your manager. These may be better suited to your interests, knowledge, and skills and they may open up sooner.

Creating a position is perhaps the best way to advance; you may be the only applicant for the job. Think about functions that your organization lacks. Define the function well and calculate the revenue-increase or cost-decrease that the function will provide to the company. Present your proposal to the executive who would manage the new function.

Lateral moves can also help your career growth and protect you from layoffs. They also broaden your experience so that you are a better candidate for promotion.

Growth can occur without changing positions. Learn everything you can about doing your current job better. Constantly invent and innovate. Add functions to your job. If these are small, just do them. If they require investment in tools or training, present a proposal to your manager. Show the benefits to the company and also to yourself. A proposal that appears to be only for the benefit of the company will not be credible.

Stay Put and Make Hay

The best option for many boomers and seniors is to remain with their current employers. Social, career, and financial benefits accrue along with vacation time. You have invested energy and time in building your knowledge of the company and its products and in establishing relationships with managers, co-workers, and subordinates. Your pension or 401K is growing, you have many opportunities to move laterally and up the ladder. For those of you who don't have this option or who seek greener pastures or new challenges, proceed to Chapters 6 and 7.

Chapter 6

Finding a New Employer

> As a job seeker two years ago, David Russo, chief people officer for Peopleclick, a Raleigh, North Carolina, recruitment-software and consulting firm, made no secret of his age when he interviewed for his current position at age 60. Mr. Russo had retired in 1999 after 19 years as head of human resources for SAS Institute Inc. and was consulting when he applied for the Peopleclick role. His graduation dates are on his résumé. His age wasn't an issue, says Mr. Russo, now 62 and glad to be working. "I thought I had a lot of juice left to help an organization."[25]

Moving On

You may be seeking a new employer because you were laid off, you moved to a new area, you love your career but not the company where you work, or you are ready to do something new and different. Finding a new position that meets your needs and wants is always a challenge. You are

---

25. Perri Capell, "*Why Some Older Executives Land Jobs -- and Others Don't*" http://www.careerjournal.com/myc/fifty/20021107-capell.html, November 7, 2002 (click on http://tinyurl.com/2lcdxz)

putting yourself in the role of a product that needs to be sold and into the role of the salesperson.

Chapter 5 was about the easiest sale: staying with your current employer. Slightly more difficult is to convince your current employer to allow you to add or try a new function. You'll need to acquire new education and skills to jump from being a nurse to working on the hospital's computer system.

Because you have ruled out staying with your current employer or are unemployed, you are now stuck between harder and hardest. Convincing a new employer to hire you for the same type of work requires normal job-hunting. Convincing a new employer to hire you in an area for which you have little experience is much more difficult.

Think seriously about moving to a new employer in your current role and then making the role switch later. Perhaps you are an accountant and you'd like to be a forest ranger. Get hired in a forest service organization as an accountant. Then start acquiring the credentials to be a ranger. Once accredited, ask your employer for the transfer. Or, you may be a technologist and would like to do fund-raising. Move into the information technology department of your favorite charity. Once you have made contacts and a contribution in that area, taking on a fund-raising role will be simpler.

If your current role is not available where you would like to work, you will need preparation and patience. Many people have successfully changed industries and companies simultaneously.

Your New Job: Shopping for Your Next Position

That's right, you are shopping. There are lots of jobs to be had even in the toughest recession. You'll be paying for your next job with your talent and time. Choose your next job more carefully than you would choose a car or house; it's the most expensive purchase you'll make!

Some job seekers are embarrassed to tell colleagues, friends and family that they are seeking employment. Remember the old adage: "Early to bed, early to rise, work like hell and advertise!" Is General Motors Corporation afraid to advertise? Microsoft Corporation? The corner grocery? Using the term "shopping" will make it clear that you are selecting your next job, not desperate for employment.

Shopping for a job is a job. You need good working conditions and a regular schedule. Your new office may be your car or a tote bag or briefcase you take on public transportation as you call on prospective employers. It may be a corner of your kitchen with a phone. It may be a computer at home, the library, or an outplacement center. In any case, it should be well organized and focused on making it the shortest job you've ever held! You don't have to take all the steps listed below or follow the thousands of pieces of advice you'll receive. If a job you want comes looking for you, snap it up!

Set your hours similar to those you'll be working when hired. If you've been going to the gym at 6am, keep it up. Don't switch to 10AM; that's a prime calling and interview time. Don't start napping or hiking in the afternoon; save those activities for the weekend as you've done in the past.

Daily and weekly goals are critical. Set minimum numbers for contacting people in your network, for meeting with people, for attending relevant events. Set small goals for applying for positions: two or three thoughtful and thorough job applications in a week is far better than twenty haphazard applications; 'spray and pray' never works.

Job Hunting Checklist

Here is a distillation of advice from dozens of successful job seekers as well as recruiters and hiring managers:

- Take a breather before you start shopping for a job. Keep it short: less than one month.

- Landing a job is a project. It's not looking for a job or finding a job. It's landing a right job, not the right job. There's more than one job that will meet your needs and wants. There are thousands that won't.

- Define what you want in a job as specifically as possible.

- Define the benefits you can bring to an employer in your ideal position.

- Now create a résumé with your ideal position as the objective and the benefit as the strengths and skills. Add the experience and education that reinforce these. Omit the items that do not contribute. For the jobs you had more than 10 years ago, write down the years of service rather than the dates.

- Identify the organizations that have filled positions like the ones you have described. Organizations can be small or medium companies/agencies/ non-profits or divisions of larger entities.

- From those companies, select the ones that are worth pursuing based on location, financial stability, and other criteria important to you.

- Obtain business cards with the job title from your objective. Yes, you can put your most recent job title on the cards. Is a teacher or a doctor who's not working any less of a teacher or a doctor? The same is true of everyone from carpenters to field service managers to zookeepers. A Manufacturing VP, a Head Buyer, and a Final Assembly Tester still hold their titles while they are in transition.

- Now create your contact list. This includes everybody you know from your most recent manager to the person that delivers your newspaper. If there are not enough industry influencers on your list, attend a conference or meeting on the topic and obtain the contact information for the speakers. If attendance is not possible, find presentations or white papers from industry influencers. Write to them with questions or comments about their presentations or papers. If they answer, they are now part of your network.

- Summarize your employment goals and the benefits you will bring an employer into a few sentences. When possible quantify results: "I mentored three students each semester". Now email this paragraph to each of your contacts or telephone them with this information, leaving voicemail if necessary. In the email, conversation, or voicemail, ask the person to notify you if he or she hears of a position where you can make a strong contribution. Thank effusively anyone who answers, even if the answer is "no." "Thank you for your prompt reply" is OK. A few days or weeks later, that person may hear of a possibility for you. For those who are more helpful, offer to return the favor.

- When an opportunity for an interview arises, schedule it far enough ahead to have time to prepare thoroughly. This means a day or two, not weeks or months. Being a little "hard to get" when it comes to interviewing is good, but too much delay could mean a missed opportunity. If an employer calls you on Monday, then schedule the interview on Wednesday or Thursday and spend all day Tuesday researching the company including talking to people who work there if appropriate.

Interviewing

Nervous about the interview? Go into it with the goal of making a friend rather than landing a job. This will help you relax and pay attention to the interviewer. Take the information you'll need for an application form, such as past employment addresses and dates. Also take two or three extra copies of your résumé. Take your business cards. You usually will receive the interviewer's card in return. That makes it easier for you to send a thank you.

Answer questions in two or three sentences. If you must give a negative answer, be sure to end on a positive note. The following are the best approaches when asked for your weaknesses:

- I have a strong sense of urgency so sometimes I am impatient with others. This has improved a lot since I started meditating.

- My first employer was very cost-conscious, so I find myself hesitating to spend company money. To combat this over-frugality, I now do a quick return-on-investment calculation.

- Occasionally I get caught up in the details. To avoid this I write a one-page summary of the project as if it's already completed. This keeps me focused on the big picture.

You may be saying "urgency, cost-consciousness, and detail-orientation" are strengths, not weaknesses! It all depends on the position, industry and company. Let's try these in the other direction:

- I like to do a thorough job and there is not always time for that approach. So I set intermediate deadlines and move on without crossing every 't' and dotting every 'i.'

- On occasion deadlines make me forget about costs. To make sure I conserve the company's money, I find at least two alternatives to every spending decision.

- I moved from advertising to accounting so I sometimes forget how critical every detail is. I now use some computer programs that check my math.

If the interviewer asks point-blank if you have specific experience or education that you lack, be very honest but avoid the word 'no'. Again, your reply should end very positively:

- That is a machine I haven't operated. It sounds similar to a machine with which I'm familiar.

- I did not pursue an MBA because I wanted a technical masters' degree. I've acquired a working knowledge of many of the MBA subjects such as marketing and finance.

- My previous employer did not require certification in that skill. I would be happy to obtain that certification if needed.

Other Job-landing Approaches

Should you bother with the traditional ways of finding a job such as answering newspaper ads, attending job fairs, or using Internet job sites? This depends on your industry. In most cases, it's a complete waste of time. If you are seeking a retail store or restaurant job, walk-ins are very effective.

I met a man in San Francisco carrying a dog-eared notebook with recipes for various interesting Cajun meals. Actually they were just lists of ingredients with no quantities or instructions. He just arrived from New Orleans and obtained job offers from two restaurants in a single day!

Should you pay for job procurement assistance? The simple answer is not until you've tried other avenues. These services are very expensive, from a few hundred dollars for clerical workers to tens of thousands for executives.

Your former employer may pay for outplacement service. Tax-supported agencies across the US and Canada provide similar services. Much of the résumé writing and interviewing skills they offer can be obtained from books that either cost a few dollars, or a trip to the library. If you need specific advice for entering a new field, it's better to obtain it from an information interview. For further details on this approach, see Homework is Critical to Success in Appendix A.

Another approach to job procurement is to join a success group of others seeking employment. This can be helpful. Choose carefully! You want a group that's dedicated to obtaining employment quickly or a group that provides general career mutual-help for both employed and unemployed members. The second type of group will meet outside normal working hours. Avoid groups that have become an end in themselves.

Big Problems

Unemployment can result in divorce or even suicide. Be very observant of your relationships with your family and friends and with your own mental state. If you see big problems arising, seek professional assistance immediately. Ask your doctor, your pastor, or your employment counselor for a referral.

You Can Do It

Landing a new job is difficult and challenging. You have been successful with more difficult tasks in the past, such as completing your education, getting a promotion, raising children, or running a marathon. Remember your past successes, think about all you have to offer, and you will be successful.

Chapter 7
Creating a New Job

Tom Jensen was laid off in the middle of the dot-com bust after a long career in mainframe computer manufacturing. He sought new employment for a few months without success. Remembering Freud's definition of insanity as doing the same thing over and over and expecting a new result, Tom took a different approach. He listed his talents and then created a free-lance music business. Tom plays in bands, teaches music, and does recording sessions for musicians. He carries three different business cards. Other than fixed time for faith and family, Tom's hours are erratic. He may approach a band at 11PM and end up creating a music CD for them in the wee hours of the next morning. When asked if he has a business plan, Tom says "positive cash flow." This means money left over after business and personal expenses including insurance and savings.[26]

---

26. Paraphrased from Tom Jensen, ProMatch Panel Discussion, November 11, 2004

The Typical Millionaire Owns a Construction Company

Although you want to work, you'd rather run your own show and not report to a manager. Take the plunge: become a consultant, contractor, or freelancer. Start or acquire a small business. Form a team and start a business that will become large. Many opportunities exist to get away from a manager without giving up a paycheck.

Entrepreneurs can end up enormously wealthy. More important than the financial benefit, though, is the joy of creating something from scratch.

Downsides? There are many. You go from having one manager to having many managers: customers, employees, investors, and vendors. Your new enterprise will require capital from a few hundred dollars to millions; some of this money will come out of your savings. You may go weeks or months without a paycheck. You may strain personal relationships or feud with your partners.

Are you cut out to take on the role of solo practitioner, business owner, or entrepreneur? You need require a sense of adventure, strong self-esteem, humor, patience, perseverance, and talent. Perhaps the most important talent is salesmanship. In the contracting, consulting, and small business worlds, often nothing happens till somebody sells something. First you have to sell the idea to your family. Then you need to sell the plan to investors. Unless it's a one-person company, you need to sell others on working for a new venture. Finally, you need to sell your product or service to prospective customers.

Free Lancer | Nearly every occupation lends itself to free-lancing. If you mowed lawns or babysat as a teen-ager, you were a free lancer. The name comes from knights who sold their services to the aristocracy. In Japan, the samurai warriors had a similar business model. Cowboys, construction workers, artists, craftsmen, doctors, attorneys, models, and realtors are often free lancers. You will be self-employed or create a corporation with yourself as the only employee. Your customers will pay you for your time or for specific tasks. You'll be responsible for employment taxes, medical insurance, and other benefits often paid by an employer. When you take a vacation or a sick day, you'll do it without pay.

So with so many downsides, why would anyone want to be a free lancer? The number one reason is that the upside is unlimited. More precisely, it's limited by your talent and time. As an employee of a larger organization, your success is limited by politics and the effort and competence of others.

Other reasons to go it alone include autonomy, time-flexibility, and working conditions. If you have problems with your manager, you can look in the mirror and tell him or her off! You can work according to your own inner clock, not the hours dictated by an employer. If you prefer to sit in your garden or the local coffee shop, that's an option. You'll save commuting time by working at home or at an office of your choosing near your home.

Almost a Free-Lancer | If you would like a little help in going out on your own, you can affiliate yourself with an organization that provides some of the infrastructure and training you'll need. If you are a hairdresser, massage therapist, personal trainer, interior designer, architect, real estate agent, stockbroker, financial planner, dentist, or one of many other occupations, you can join a group of similar people or rent a spot in a company. You'll still run the show and have nearly unlimited potential income. While you'll need to pay fees or a percentage of your revenues to the organization, these costs will provide you training, mentoring, facilities, and other assistance. The biggest benefit will be a community of professional colleagues.

Small Business Owner Another way to run the show is to create or purchase a small business: retail store (bricks-and-mortar, art-fair or Internet-based), dry-cleaning establishment, automobile service, janitorial service, or the like.) With nearly a billion boomers and seniors world-wide, any business that meets the needs of people 40 and over has high profit potential. Think in terms of exercise studios, adventure travel, teeth whitening, home-safety, gardening supplies, pet services/goods, and more.

Like freelancing, owning a small business has advantages and disadvantages:

Table 7-1:

Advantages of owning a small business	Disadvantages of owning a small business
You run the show.	You need to find and retain competent, reliable employees at a reasonable cost.
You set the hours of operation.	You need to set and maintain hours that meet the competition.
Your profits are potentially unlimited.	Your potential losses can be very high.
Many of your normal expenses will be tax-deductible.	You'll be subject to a number of business taxes and fees; also, you'll need business insurance.
You'll become known in the community; people will listen to your opinions on community issues.	You'll be constantly asked for donations of your time and money.

You can think of the disadvantages as challenges.

To become a small business owner, you can buy a franchise, buy a small business, or start your own small business. Which of these routes you select will depend on the type of businesses that interest you, the amount of capital you have, and your level of expertise. Buying a franchise takes the most money and the least amount of experience. Buying an existing small business or a franchise location already in operation carries the least risk.

If you have very little money to invest and lots of knowledge, starting a home-based business is the best approach for you. Converting a creative hobby into a business is one method. Many such businesses are now selling the fruits of their labors on eBay Inc. and receive orders from all over the world.[27]

One of the best ways to be successful is to do the opposite of the other providers. If most of the restaurants in your neighborhood are fast-food franchises, you can provide an alternative: a neighborhood table service café. A similar approach can work for grocery stores, exercise studios, and maid services. On the other hand, if the businesses near you are high-end and costly, your approach might be to provide a budget offering. Do your market research and be sure that there are customers for your dream business.

Entrepreneur-ship

An entrepreneur starts a small business with the intention of growing it. Unlike the small business owner who buys or builds a dry cleaning service, the entrepreneur starts a chain of dry cleaners. He doesn't just sell his handy dandy new device, but gets it patented and creates a manufacturing company. The entrepreneur may start out alone but sooner or later will be part of a management team. The business can be self-funded or you can seek angel or venture capital investors. The entrepreneur and the investors may be building a

---

27. Jacky Hood, Email exchange with Barbara Shaughnessy, December, 2006

business that will last for decades or centuries. In order to obtain a return on their investment of time and money, they need a business that will be bought out or become a public corporation in a few years. Because the risks are high in starting new enterprises, the potential financial gain must be much greater than traditional investments. A venture capital firm will want its investment to be increased by one or two orders of magnitude in a few years.

Entrepreneurs are passionate about the product or service they will provide. They are persistent and persuasive. If these words describe you, there is no better way to cap your career than by creating a new company.

Robert Weiner, a longstanding arthritis sufferer, created the HanDee Soapsacks™ as a means to handle and manipulate a bar of soap throughout his showering routine.[28]

Another Advantage of Going It Alone

Finding new employment after being out of work for a while can be daunting. Employers simply do not trust gaps in your employment history. Perhaps they think you were in prison or on a long vacation. As a self-employed contractor or consultant or as a business owner or entrepreneur, those gaps fill in easily. Suppose you are laid off and spend months looking for a new position. Then you start a new venture for a year or two. Later, it doesn't work out and you decide to look for a job. The entire time you are

---

28. Barbara Mascio, "*Why Seniors become entrepreneurs - or* Senior-Preneurs" in Working Seniors - Healthier Seniors http://www.bestdirectory.us/articledirectory.php?CatID=28&ArtID=47543 (click on http://tinyurl.com/3by2qn, June 16, 2006

Same Job, New Job or New Enterprise

out of work can be attributed to deciding on the new venture, mapping it out, and then running it for a while.

No matter which route you choose, working for pay will keep you young. But that's not all; you can also have the benefits of retirement while still working. The next chapter shows how to do this.

Chapter 8: Equal Time

Al Wallace worked as an engineer and manager well beyond early retirement. During part of that time, Al commuted 29 miles from Menlo Park to Alameda. Because of his knowledge of specialized electronic circuitry, Al was very valuable to his employer. Yet Al also spent dozens of hours practicing and playing the clarinet and flute. He performed in several combos and always spent a week each year at jazz camp. Al finally retired from electronics when faced with training yet another boss. Now music is Al's major occupation; he is paid for his performances and volunteers as a teacher of disadvantaged students. He still goes to jazz camp every year.[29]

Doing It All

Retirement beckons because all of us want more time for ourselves, our causes, and our friends and families. With a little planning, you can work full-time and still have an active personal and social life. Chances are you will do more non-work activities than your retired colleagues and friends.

---

29. Jacky Hood, Interview of Al Wallace, November 12, 2006

One Hundred (Useful) Hours in Every Week

A math professor who also trains as a gymnast and cares for a senile mathematician was asked how he does it. The answer: "There are 168 hours in every week." A corollary is that there are 100 useful hours in every week. The others are spent sleeping, eating, grooming, maintaining homes and cars, and commuting. If you are efficient with these life necessities, you may have even more than 100 useful hours in a week.

So how much time does a full-time job consume? Nominally 40 hours, but let's assume that you put in some extra time and crank that up to 50. You will still have 50 hours a week for all the things you want to do.

Perhaps you work for an organization where people regularly work more than 50 hours each week. Law firms and high-technology companies are notorious for expecting 80 or more hours of work from salaried employees. The reluctance of older workers to put in so much time is one of the excuses companies give for seeking younger workers. However, older workers have the wisdom to use their time well. Junior workers put in 80 hours one week, then need 80 hours the following week to correct mistakes.

If asked in a job interview about your willingness to work long hours, a good answer is "I believe in working hard and playing hard." Say that you are always willing to pitch in during an emergency and you believe in preventing emergencies. Ken Oshman, CEO of Echelon Corporation, once said "If people are consistently working more than 40 hours per week, we are doing something wrong."

When you start a new job, project, or consulting/contracting assignment, the first two weeks set the pattern. Demonstrate that you can leave at 4 PM and still make a strong contribution. Also try to get the long-hour practice changed for the benefit of everyone. Point out to the employer that the working practices are discriminating against people with children at home and thereby limiting the talent pool available.

If you really do have to be at meetings into the late afternoon and early evening, then take time earlier in the day to do the things you love: go for a hike at dawn or at lunchtime. Read a novel at the local coffee shop mid-morning. Meet friends or family for lunch. Visit a museum mid-afternoon.

Hourly and other non-exempt workers usually have fixed hours; this can be both a disadvantage and an advantage. You have less freedom to join friends and family for specific events. You also work only 40 hours per week and have 60 hours for all your other pursuits. If overtime is available, you can often choose whether to take it and you are paid extra for that choice. You can use that money to supplement your savings or have even more fun the following week.

Something Special Every Week

If you always use your 50 hours of free time per week for the same activities, every week will be the same. A middle-aged man received a wakeup call about his own life when his brother died suddenly. He looked at his own health and decided he would live at least ten more years. He purchased 1000 marbles for the approximately 1000 Saturdays in those ten years. The next thing he did was cancel his golf game for the following Saturday. His wife was astounded and asked about the cancellation. The man answered, "I've played at least 200 rounds of golf with that group and can't remember more than 2 or 3 of the games." Instead he invited all of his nieces and nephews for a Saturday breakfast that he did remember. Then he removed one marble from the jar. Each Saturday for 10 years, he found something new and interesting to do. Recently he started at his next 1000 marbles and 10 years of doing something special every week.

In career workshops, I distribute notebooks with 52 dividers (two sets of alphabetical dividers work nicely). The cover of the notebook shows a wrapped gift. Each week is a gift, the precious present.

Something Special Nearly Every Day

Some days are consumed by work and chores. But most days there's time for something special: planning a vacation, stopping by the library, watching an excellent movie, or calling a friend.

Time Management

Make a list of all the things you must do. Now cross out half of them! Stop seeing people you dislike and volunteering for organizations that don't appreciate you. Clean your house or wash your car half as often. At the office, cancel half the standing meetings or make them into true standing meetings: ones in which people are not allowed to sit! It's amazing how much faster people come to decisions on their feet. Take the chairs and tables out of the conference rooms and install elbow-height counters.

Documents are a big time sink. You read them, lay them down, pick them up, read them again, stash them, lose them, and search for them, on and on. Obtain some file folders and a big box or filing cabinet. Handle each piece of paper only once. Put a recycling bin next to your mailbox. Deposit junk mail, envelopes, and stuffers as soon as you collect the mail. Pay bills immediately and then file the statement. Put magazines in a to-be-read file. If the previous issue of that magazine is still unread, recycle it.

Material possessions also consume much of our time. We dust them and move them around. Throw away or give away and stop buying things. Obtain books from the library. You can also check out albums, tapes, and DVDs or rent them. Have only a few pots, pans, and dishes and use them every day. Reduce the quantities of towels and bed linens you own. Look in your closet; if you haven't worn a garment in a year, chuck it.

Soon you'll find you can live in a smaller home and save time on house and yard maintenance.

Save time and money on dry cleaning by washing inexpensive garments; if washing ruins them, throw them away. The money and time saved more than make up for the cost. Save time on haircuts; get your hair cut less often or cut it yourself. Save time on shopping by ordering through catalogs or online. Shop in your own pantry or closet.

Now the fun part of time management: make a list of the things you want to do: travel to Spain, learn to play the harp, paint the guest room, visit that new restaurant, and invite friends for brunch. Pin this list on your bulletin board. Put these items on your calendar; treat these appointments as seriously as a visit to the dentist.

Double Your Fun: Doing What You Want 100 Hours Per Week

The absolutely best way to do the things you love while holding a full-time job is to find a job you love. Dave and Sheila Mills are now 63 years old. Their job, hobby, and love are leading river-rafting tours on the Salmon River in Idaho. Roger Smith started volunteering as a girls' volleyball coach when his daughter was in middle school. Now the daughter is in graduate school and Roger is the owner and manager of a volleyball club.

Final Message

You can have it all: autonomy, income, and free time. Work hard, play hard, and love your life. Be paid for your effort, talent, and wisdom and live every precious minute to the fullest and stay young.

Appendix A: The Reality of Retirement

> Our venture capital climate started with successful entrepreneurs who disliked retirement.[30]

Dream Retirements Down the Drain

Asked what they plan to do in retirement; many people have vague dreams of pursuing leisure activities all day every day. They love their evenings, weekends, and vacations and feel that traveling, sports, hobbies, and social activities will fill their days. Once they retire, they find they cannot afford this plan, cannot find others who want to join them, and find that the activities are far less enjoyable when constantly pursued. It's like only having dessert for every meal. Leisure activities are enjoyable because they provide a change and a reward for productive work.

---

30. Terry E. Bibbens, *Encouraging and Expanding Entrepreneurship*, http://www.sba.gov/ADVO/laws/test01_0301.txt

How do People Really Spend their Time in Retirement?

Researchers John Robinson and Geoffrey Godbey found that, on average, men over 65 have 8 hours more free time per week than their counterparts aged 55-64. Unfortunately, these men used seven of those hours to watch more television. Women in the older group had five more hours of free time but watched four more hours of television than younger women.[31]

Why so much Television Viewing?

Why do retired people spend so much time watching television? Is it because the programs bring enjoyment? "Turning on the TV set and withdrawing from the world is not a sign that a senior is content,"[32] says Arthur Koenig, author of Purpose and Power in Retirement. "It more often signals depression and disappointment." Television viewing is the most passive non-sleeping activity humans pursue. Unfortunately, it is also highly addictive because of the alpha waves produced by the brain. People deprived of television viewing showing addiction withdrawal symptoms.

Quiet activities such as reading, conversing, writing, and solitary games show more mental activity. However, repetitive games of solitaire or Sudoku or low-level crossword puzzles or reading can also be signs of withdrawing from life. They may even indicate depression. When Novelist/philosopher Ayn Rand became depressed in middle age, she spent hours playing solitaire.

---

31. John Robinson and Geoffrey Godbey, *Time for Life: The Surprising, Ways Americans Use Their Time*, Pennsylvania State University, Press, University Park, PA, 1997
32. Arthur Koeni, "*Purpose and Power in Retirement*"

Constant eating is another activity that may signal loneliness or boredom and can create health problems. Weight gain in retired people is common. It results from both overeating and lack of physical activity. Like people of any age, non-working adults may use food to compensate for lack of purpose or interpersonal relationships.[33]

Life-Threatening Addictions

While television viewing represents a slow form of death, many retirees become addicted to more immediate poisons: drugs, alcohol, gambling, and crime.

Although the use of alcohol and other drugs generally declines as people grow older, problems with alcohol use among older adults (people age 60 and older) pose a health and safety risk for many and a serious concern to their families. As the baby boom generation ages, the problem will loom larger on the social agenda. Research studies have documented the phenomenon known as "late-onset alcoholism." In one clinical study, at least 41 percent of the people age 65 and over who were enrolled in a Mayo Clinic alcohol treatment program reported that their alcohol problems began after age 60. Data on late-onset alcohol abuse gathered in other studies provides further evidence that one's alcohol consumption may not be consistent across time; some people may increase their consumption as a response to age-related stresses such as the loss of employment, widowhood, or other bereavement.[34]

---

33. http://www.msnbc.msn.com/id/7222053/; Seniors strive to keep off retirement pounds, CDC: More than 70% are overweight. By Tom Costello Correspondent NBC News Updated: 5:09 p.m. PT March 17, 2005

As many as one in six Americans 60 and older are over dependent on alcohol. Twenty percent of the elderly who are admitted to psychiatric wards show symptoms of alcoholism or substance abuse. By some estimates, alcoholism today rivals heart attacks as a killer of senior citizens. A growing type of abuser is the "late-onset alcoholic," according to author Susan Abrams, an Illinois law graduate who is the clerk for US District Judge Harold A. Baker in Central Illinois. Such a person shows no sign of alcoholism until major physical or lifestyle changes, such as health problems, death of a spouse, financial worries, depression, or sleeplessness, trigger overdrinking after age 50. Prescription and over-the-counter drug abuse also increase with advancing age. While some seniors turn to alcohol, others turn to antidepressant medications. Fifty percent of all sedatives are used by people over the age of 59.[35]

A job or career will not cure every case of addiction or indolence. However, in many cases it will prevent these situations from arising.

Will Volunteer Work Create A Successful Retirement?

To promote a happy retirement, volunteer work needs to:

- Be challenging

34. "*Seniors and Alcohol*", West Virginia University Alcohol Awareness Site http://www.hsc.wvu.edu/som/cmed/alcohol/alcoholism/seniors.htm (click on http://tinyurl.com/2zu8x8)

35. Alcohol Abuse: Senior-citizen drinking problems labeled 'invisible epidemic' Mark Reutter, Business Editor, News Bureau, University of Illinois at Urbana-Champaign http://www.news.uiuc.edu/gentips/02/05alcohol.html

- Be performed in a professional setting away from home
- Be long-lasting
- Offer learning opportunities
- Have an organizational structure with executives, managers, and support staff
- Provide promotion paths
- Have low turnover so long-term relationships can be formed
- Be difficult to quit
- Have punctuality and attendance expectations
- Have performance and goal metrics at every level.

All of these factors are normal in paying jobs and very rare in volunteer work. They all contribute to mental health. In order to have some of the physical health benefits of paid work, the volunteer organization needs fitness facilities, classes and encouragement. Some volunteer work, such as lifeguarding and trail building, meets this need.

Impossible for any volunteer work to provide are the wealth benefits of working: salary, paid vacations, medical insurance, tuition reimbursements, and other compensation.

The best way to avoid an unhappy retirement, is to avoid retirement altogether. Keep working. If you care about a cause, get a job in that field, volunteer in your non-working hours, donate money, or put the cause in your will.

Appendix B: Overcoming Age Discrimination

> Two campers in the forest have just woken up and are walking around their campsite barefoot. Suddenly they see a bear running towards them. One of the campers starts putting his running shoes on. The other camper says "There's no point putting your shoes on, because you can't run faster than a bear." The first camper replies "I don't have to run faster than the bear; I just have to run faster than you."[36]

Discrimination: Both Real and Imaginary

'Discrimination' was once a proud accomplishment. A person with discriminating taste sought only the best associates, reading matter, and so forth. Unfortunately, the term is now associated with stereotyping the members of a group. For boomer and senior workers the negative stereotypes are inflexibility, lack of innovation, unwillingness to work hard or long, frequent illnesses and absences, high salary and benefit expectations and costs, and mark time until retirement.

---

36. Philip Dorrell reciting an old joke, http://www.1729.com/blog/WeakUserPasswords.html

As with all stereotypes, there is some truth in these generalizations. Some experienced people are marking time. Some boomers and seniors have health problems and related absences. Health insurance companies charge higher premiums if employees are older. For example,[37]

- Age 25: $161 per month
- Age 40: $320 per month
- Age 55: $736 per month

In this example, the employer would be paying nearly four times as much for health insurance if the average age of its employees were 55 rather than 25.

Similarly, older workers do have more experience and therefore expect higher salaries.

Two Approaches

Overcoming real or imagined age discrimination requires either exuding youthful qualities or capitalizing on your age and experience. You can combine these approaches for optimum success in job responsibilities, in compensation, and, if needed, in securing a new position.

In one of my Third Stage classes, I split the group in two. The teams were asked to debate the value of showing versus hiding their age on the job or in job hunting. Though the members of one team were expected to take the "hide" position, they refused! Everyone in the class felt that any

---

37. http://www.tdi.state.tx.us/CONSUMER/sergcdallas.html (click on http://tinyurl.com/2raecy)

type of deception is wrong. As much as I admire the participants' integrity, I still believe in putting the best foot forward. Any jobholder or job seeker should display energy, enthusiasm, and creativity while downplaying boredom, illnesses, and other negatives. It's the same as combing your hair before going to work.

Remember, good posture and a smile are as effective as liposuction and facelifts – and less expensive.

Salary Discrimination vs. Age Discrimination

The most common advice on avoiding age discrimination is to convince employers that you are willing to work for a low salary. Doing this makes some sense (but not much) only in these situations:

- You are switching fields.

- There are no jobs available at your desired salary.

Unless you live in a very remote area or are in a field with low demand, there are far more openings than you have time to pursue thoroughly. The operative word here is 'thoroughly.' Two or three job applications per week are enough per Chapter 6.

So you need to filter the jobs using various criteria. Unconsciously, you'll be filtering on geography, fit with your background, company reputation, and so forth. Simply make salary one of the gating criteria. Remember, these are the filters. Once they are applied you look at the important factors such as responsibility, challenge, and opportunity. These are the factors you mention in your cover letters, on your résumé and in job interviews. The question of salary should not arise because you have already eliminated positions with low salaries.

If you have been a manager of technicians, choose only openings at that level or above. Do not apply for technician or senior technician jobs. They will be more difficult for you to attain (because you'll be considered "overqualified" and unlikely to stay). If you do get such a job, you'll take a salary cut, and you'll be frustrated.

You're not seeing jobs in the newspapers, at job fairs, or on the Internet at your level? Of course not. Companies fill postings in the least expensive, least risky fashion. First they look inside for candidates. Second, they ask employees for referrals. Third, they post jobs on their own web sites. (Some refrain from posting any jobs because it provides too much information about their strategic direction to their competitors.) Fourth, they troll for résumés on posting sites. Next they hire recruiters on a contingency basis, paying them only if an ideal candidate is hired and stays several months.

Only as a last resort will companies pay money to attract prospects: bounties for employee referrals, newspaper ads, and Internet job sites. The jobs that reach these levels are those for which there are many openings (factory workers, junior engineers, junior accountants). This way the recruiting cost per position is lower. For very senior positions, companies use retained recruiters and usually keep the searches confidential.

So how do you find openings at your level and above that also meet your geography and industry requirements? More importantly, how do you make it easy for prospective employers to find you?

- Tell everyone you know, from your gardener to the CEO of your target company, that you are talented and available.
- Post your profile, résumé, or both on many job boards.
- Attend professional events and exchange business cards, especially with the presenters.
- Set up meetings with the people you meet at these events as well as with former managers, customers, and suppliers.
- Write a survey article for your field, interviewing executives and managers to obtain the content. If you cannot find a journal or magazine that will publish it, do so yourself in the form of a white paper that you include with your résumé and on your personal Web site.

Even if you are changing fields, you do not need to accept an entry-level salary. Much of your experience is portable. Planning, organizing, negotiating, economizing, and innovating apply in any field. Certain disciplines such as accounting, finance, human resources, customer service, sales, and information technology are found in all industries. Emphasize all your knowledge and skill and downplay specifics of the industry you are leaving. Learn about your new industry through journals, Web sites, conferences, and interviews (such as the ones you'll do to write that article!)

Avoid the Kindergarten | Some companies want only twenty-somethings. Skip them. Not only will you be wasting your time, they won't last long without adult supervision.

Fields that Love Gray Hair | Education, training, consulting, and financial services are fields that require and reward experience. It's such a pleasure to apply and interview for positions in these areas. Be sure to be up-to-date as well as experienced.

Homework is Critical to Success | Before you approach any company, research it thoroughly. Learn everything you can about its products, services, market performance, competitors, and customers. Study the profiles of its executives. Find out its involvement in the community and in the wider world.

The job you want in the company is probably not posted on its Web site. Nevertheless, you should read all the job descriptions on that site even if there are dozens. What employee characteristics are cited often? Do you sense a bias toward experience? Great. If you see an emphasis on high energy and flexibility in candidates and many mentions of a demanding fast-paced environment, you may want to drop this target company. It's not that you lack energy and flexibility, it's because these phrases are euphemisms for young workers. (The irony is that working conditions like this are more likely to discourage people in their 20s and 30s with children rather than boomers or seniors.)

For the companies that are still on your target list, try to find people in the company with whom you can talk. Your goal is not to ask for a job but to determine the company culture. A telephone conversation is helpful; a visit is ten times better. For example, the rumors here in Silicon Valley are that Yahoo! Inc. hires only very young people. Recently a 50-something colleague of mine who works for Yahoo invited me to lunch in the Yahoo cafeteria. Either the rumors are blatantly wrong or it was "Bring Your Parents to Work" day. There were people ranging from 20 to over 70 in the cafeteria.

Take the Plunge

You've now stacked the odds in your favor by choosing a company that values experience and is likely to open jobs in the near future at your current level or higher. You've learned as much as possible about the company. Now:

- Articulate to yourself how you can contribute to the firm. Condense this into a few sentences to use in cover letters and interviews. Plan this out for 2 or 3 years. Think about the first, second, and third things you can accomplish: showing XYZ Company how to expand its residential business into additional neighborhoods, adding commercial accounts to the customer base, and mentoring new-hires in efficiencies and customer service. In another situation you might apply wireless technology to the current operation, create cost savings, and help the company balance its month-to-month inventory swings.

- Structure your résumé around the company, the industry, and the contribution you can make. De-emphasize everything else.

- Emphasize your recent experience: no more than ten years. Omit everything earlier. (The only exception is if you are trying to return to a field in which you worked earlier. It's best to make that earlier experience part of the summary at the beginning of the résumé without mentioning dates.)

- Choose the personal details that emphasize energy and enthusiasm. Cross-country skiing is better than gardening. Volunteer fund-raising is better than simply belonging to a service club.

- Show a desire for promotion in your stated objective, the first item after your name. For example: "Objective: Trainer of helicopter mechanics leading to supervisor of other trainers." This indicates that you are not marking time until retirement.

Once You Are Hired

The first two weeks on the job set the pattern. Demonstrate that you can leave at 4 PM and still make a strong contribution. Junior workers put in 80 hours one week, then need 80 hours the following week to correct mistakes.

Appendix C
Boomer/Senior Career Paths and Boosters

The career paths of boomers and seniors represent a new frontier. People travel these paths for 10 to 40 years or more. Many paths represent the next leg of a journey that began decades in the past. Other paths are new routes.

Some boomer/senior career paths are more narrow and uphill. These include promotions and increasing responsibilities. Others become increasingly wider roads as the individual broadens knowledge, skills, and contributions to an industry or community.

Companies, non-profits, and other organizations that recognize, facilitate, and encourage boomer/senior career paths will win in the marketplace and make large, long-lasting contributions to the economy and culture. Their talented, experienced, and diverse workforces will ensure their success.

We are collecting and documenting success stories and publishing Boomer/Senior Boosters: organizations committed to hiring, developing, and promoting boomers and seniors. If you know of organizations that meet these criteria, please write to jacky.hood@bigtent.info. Please include a second email address or a telephone number in case a spam filter blocks our reply.

In this Appendix, we describe a few of the Boomer/Senior Boosters we have collected. Because our audience is global, we are including large national and international companies. However, many Boomer/Senior Boosters are regional or local; be sure to look in your own area. Here is an example of a smaller Boomer/Senior Booster:

With one-third of his 75 employees age 50 or over, Brian Hughes is already living in the world of 2010. By then, nearly a third of the U.S. work force will have had 50 or more birthdays, according to a report by AARP. That's OK with the vice president and great-grandson of the founder of Hughes Environmental Engineering Inc., a $16 million Montvale, New Jersey, heating and air conditioning service firm. Hughes, 37, interviews people who are nearing retirement as readily as the freshly graduated. And, he says, "the older guy's probably going to get the job." Companies have to learn to hire, keep and appreciate over-50 employees because they are increasingly becoming available. "It's a matter of necessity," says Hughes. "There's not enough talent in our industry to fill the jobs."

Mark Henricks, "Hiring employees over age 50 Is a smart move—if you do it right". Entrepreneur Magazine[38], October 2006.

Here are some Boomer/Senior Boosters who operate on the national or international level:

---

38. http://www.entrepreneur.com/magazine/entrepreneur/2006/october/167826.html (click on http://tinyurl.com/34y54y)

American Express Company	American Express is a global payments, network, and travel company. Its products and services include global card network services; charge card and credit cards for consumers and businesses; consumer and small business lending products; American Express travelers checks and gift cards; merchant acquiring and transaction processing; business expense management products and services; consumer travel services; and business travel and travel management services. **Ameriprise Financial Advisors** is another Boomer/Senior Booster that is now completely separate from American Express. Ameriprise employs more than 12,000 financial advisors and registered representatives. Many are boomers and seniors who enjoy strong career opportunities.
CVS Pharmacy, Home Depot, Saks Inc., Toys "R" Us	CVS Pharmacy, Home Depot, Saks Inc., Toys "R" Us are large retailers. They are so serious about career paths that they have joined with the U.S. Department of Labor and the NRF Foundation to create three National Professional Certifications: Customer Service, Sales, and Management. The certifications use modern computer-based training methods. The American Express Foundation contributed to this effort. Here is the Web site[39] for the Management Certification:
EDO Corporation	EDO Corporation designs and manufactures a range of products for defense, intelligence, and commercial markets, and provides related engineering and professional services. Major

---

39. http://www.nrf.com/con-tent/default.asp?folder=foundation&file=Manage-mentcert.htm (click on http://tinyurl.com/2zgqg4)

product groups include defense electronics, communications, aircraft-armament systems, undersea warfare systems, integrated composite structures, and professional and engineering services. Recently it acquired CAS Inc. and Impact Science & Technology Inc. EDO's youngest officer is 48; several are in their 60s. In 2005, the employees of EDO Corporation contributed a total of $126,489 towards Hurricane Katrina relief efforts. For other examples of how companies and their employees can contribute to the betterment of society, see Chapter 4: "*Working for a Cause.*"

Fujitsu Limited

Fujitsu Limited, headquartered in Kanagawa, Japan, is an information technology company. The company operates in three business segments. The Technology Solution segment manufactures and sells products such as servers, storage systems, network management systems, and optical transport systems, as well as providing system integrations service, network service, and system support service. The Ubiquitous Product Solution segment offers products such as personal computers, mobile phones, hard disk drives, magnetic optical discs, as well as optical transmitter and receiver modules. The Device Solution segment is engaged in the manufacture and sale of large-scale-integrated semiconductor packages, relays and connectors, among others. Employees number 150,000 worldwide.

We congratulate these forward-looking companies and organizations.

May all your pathways bring you joy.

About the Author

Jacky Hood became an engineer when few women entered the profession. She rode a bicycle across North America at the age of 41. Her mother retired at 81; Jacky intends to work even longer. She is a management consultant and teaches classes on career strategy, customer service, corporate governance, and business management. Her clients include Philips Medical, RAE Systems, Ellie Mae, Sun Microsystems, and many other firms. Jacky has held management positions at Hewlett-Packard, SlamDunk Networks, IBM/ROLM, and other companies. She is CEO of FieldDay Solutions and an instructor at Chalk Institute, Foothill College, and UC Santa Cruz Extension. This is Jacky's fourth book.

Success Stories

During the research and writing of this book, we collected many success stories. Twelve of these stories appear in this book on the pages shown:

Contributor	Page#
Adrian, Pat	45
Franklin, Frederic	51
Glass, Dorothea	38
Jensen, Tom	67
Mills, Dave and Sheila	80
Rosten, Frank	37
Russo, David	57
Scheiber, Anne	13
Vance, Rita	38
Wallace, Al	75
Weiner, Robert	73

We plan to publish more success stories in the future. Please let us know if you or someone you know is a boomer or senior who has returned to school, found a new job, become a consultant or contractor, started a company, or been promoted in the past five years. Write to jacky.hood@bigtent.info.

Please include a second email address or a telephone number in case our reply to you runs into a spam filter. If you nominate someone else, please obtain permission from the nominee and include the nominee's contact information.

Books

Purchase these books at Happy About http://happyabout.info or at other online and physical bookstores.

Is it who or what one knows that makes the difference? Both!

'Tales From The Networking Community' gives you tips, techniques and shares anecdotal stories that will help you succeed with your networking goals.

Paperback $19.95 80pgs
eBook $11.95 82pgs

Find a life that fits your dreams

This book speaks to the the well-established business leader who has achieved success and now wants to somehow fit a life into those dreams.

Paperback $19.95 148pgs
eBook $11.95 150pgs

Settle your IRS debt for pennies on the dollar and save thousands in professional fees!

With this book, you can make an Offer in Compromise with the same software tool used by the pros.

Paperback $174.95 308pgs
eBook $154.95 310pgs

This book delivers Enjoyment, Motivation and Permission!

After losing her family legacy, Evelyn Preston is cajoled into earning a securities license to make up her personal investment losses.

Paperback $19.95 312pgs
eBook $11.95 314pgs

Turn Your Visions into Reality!

This book combines both the biblical and business principles with practical experience to allow you to fulfill your 'true' purpose in life.

Paperback $19.95 116pgs
eBook $11.95 117pgs

Live the life you were meant to live!

The 30day Bootcamp: Your Ultimate Life Makeover is a step-by-step program that will teach you all of the tips, tricks, and techniques you need to get back in the driver's seat of your life.

Paperback $19.95 248pgs
eBook $11.95 250pgs

www.ingramcontent.com/pod-product-compliance
Ingram Content Group UK Ltd.
Pitfield, Milton Keynes, MK11 3LW, UK
UKHW021303180426
11947UKWH00015B/999